TEXAS
LIMESTONE II

A Climber's Guide

COVER PHOTO: Paul Clark on Concentrics (5.12); photo by Jeff Jackson.

TEXAS
LIMESTONE II
A Climber's Guide

Text by Jeff Jackson
Topos and Maps by Kevin Gallagher
Layout by Rebecca Gonzales
Cover by Max Hoberman

Homo Aggro Press
Austin, Texas
1995

"There are two sorts of guidebooks; those that are read before and those
that are to be read after and the ones that are to be read after the fact
are bound to be incomprehensible to a certain extent before; if the fact
is of enough importance in itself. So with any book on mountain ski-ing,
sexual intercourse, wing shooting, or any other thing which is impossible to
make come true on paper . . . it being always an individual experience,
there comes a place in the guidebook where you must say do not come
back until you have ski-ed, had sexual intercourse, shot quail or grouse,
or been to the bullfight so that you will know what we are talking about.
So from now on it is inferred that you have been to the bullfight."
— Ernest Hemingway, *Death in the Afternoon*

Acknowledgments: Alex Catlin, Norman Chu, Paul Clark, Wayne Crill, James Crump, Benji Fink, Paul Irby, Cristina Jackson, Christian "Yogaman" Leeby, "Lucky" Mike Kline, Jimmy Menendez, Jack Mileski, Rich Pollard, Russell and Karen Rand, John Southrey, Rick Watson, Barry "Bluebeard" Wilson and all Texas Climbers.

Special thanks to our **Sponsors:** Mack "Maxtron" Hargrave, La Sportiva, Metolius, Esprit Ropes, Inc. and PrAna for the duds.

Disclaimer: This guide to Texas Limestone is not intended to be a complete guide to all the limestone in Texas. The authors have discovered and hoarded too many crags to believe we could track down all the limestone climbing out there. If you would like to see your favorite area in the next edition of this guide please write to Limestone P. O. Box 49894 Austin, Texas 78765.

Warning: It's not our fault if you fall down. Don't use this guide in place of judgement. Judgement is an inherent quality that tells the climber when to push on, when to back off and when to go home. Not everyone possesses good judgment. If you don't possess good judgement, don't purchase this guide. Don't take up rock climbing. Take up gym climbing. Rock climbing is by its very nature a potentially hazardous activity which, when practiced by those lacking sound judgement results in messy accidents and/or death. CLIMB AT YOUR OWN RISK!!!!

" 'Have no fear!' said the cat. 'I will not let you fall. I will hold you up high as I stand on a ball. With a book on one hand! And a cup on my hat! But that is not all I can do!' said the cat. 'Look at me! Look at me! Look at me now! It is fun to have fun but you have to know how.' That is what the cat said . . . Then he fell on his head!"

—Dr. Seuss, *The Cat In The Hat*

Apologies: If I've learned anything by climbing in Texas for almost twenty years, it's that climbers around here are a cantankerous lot. The authors would like to apologize right now to the people we've pissed off just by publishing this guide. We'd like to apologize for any butt-clenching that goes on because of offensive language. We'd like to apologize for leaving your name out of this guide. For getting first ascent information wrong. For getting you lost. For sandbagging ratings. For grade inflation. For poor topos. For leaving out your secret area. For including your secret area. For long-winded digressions. For misrepresenting the facts. For making stuff up. For being too silly.

"Does the author expect to make money by it? It'll be a marvel if he gets any, for it will be nothing but hurry, hurry, like a tailor on Easter Eve; and work that's done in haste is never finished as perfectly as it ought to be. Let this Master Moor, or whatever he is, take care and look what he is doing, for I and my master will provide him with enough rubble in the way of adventures and different things for him to be able to make up not only a second part but a hundred more."

— Sancho Panza, *Don Qiuxote*

Preface to the 2nd Edition

Can you remember a time when there was no Texas Limestone, a climber's guide? Picture a world without that useful index of all your favorite climbs. No cheesy Indian on the cover. No not-so-great photos. No baffling topos. No Zee mono gunner. No Frederick's— not Nietzsche, not Remmington. No Jack Mileski. No slander (see Mt. Bonnell).

It couldn't happen. But it did. At this time last year the booming mills at Homo Aggro Press were silenced and the last copy of Central Texas Limestone, a climber's guide , was laid to rest in the cavernous halls of REI's warehouse facility in Sumner, WA.

The authors celebrated the success of their book by dividing the profits, flying to Las Vegas and blowing hundreds of thousands of dollars on cheap liquor and sin. Scared, penniless and psychologically broken, they crawled back into town a month ago begging for a job.

I knew it would happen. I can see right through those good-for-nothing slackers. So when they told me they'd never write another guidebook, I just chuckled and nodded. Too much work, they said. Everybody is a critic. The topo's are too hard to draw. I don't know how to spell.

I'd heard it all before. It was the typical litany of a soft-bellied sport-climber. Save those excuses for your pathetic redpoint attempts, boys, I said, and get to work. I don't want to see hide nor hair of ye until the book is done.

I worked them without mercy. Everyday it was up at ten and on the rock by eleven, climbing hundreds of new routes at dozens of new crags. Voluminous notetaking. Phone calls. Scrawled maps and topos. Beer, pizza and Ligatend.

Finally, it was done. Texas Limestone II was born, the proud guidebook you now hold in your hands. Expanded, beautifully written and photographed, logically arranged and packed with significance— it is everything a guidebook should be and then some. If you are standing at the store, glancing through this book, I can only urge you to buy it. It is the single greatest investment you'll ever make. Good things happen to people who buy this book. A man in Indiana bought this book for his daughter and a young woman, blind since birth, miraculously regained her sight in Coral Gabels, Florida. Another man, disgusted by a sandbagged rating, threw this book into the Sano-Can at Reimer's Ranch. He later broke his ankle while bouldering at the Hueco Tanks.

I'm not trying to scare you. I'm just giving you the gospel truth. BUY THIS BOOK! And when something good happens to you, don't thank the authors.

Thank me,
Mr. X
CEO Homo Aggro Press

What is Homo Aggro?
Australopithicus, Homo Habilis, Homo Africanus, Neanderthal, Homo Erectus, Homo Sapien, Homo Aggro. Aggressive Man. The next step in the evolutionary chain. A man so highly developed he/she can rifle logarithmic equations while sending 5.15.

Table of Contents

Introduction

Dallas Rock

Bouldering — Plano Pyramids	11
Bouldering — Renner Road	11
Bouldering — Matilda Bridge	13
Bouldering — Trammel Trestle	13
Bouldering — Tietze Park	15
Bouldering — Malone Wall	15
Mineral Wells	15
Cleburn/Chisolm Wall	20

Houston Rock?

Temple/Belton Limestone

Miller Springs	30
Morgan's Point	34

Georgetown Limestone

The Riverside Sanctuary	35
Bouldering — Blue Hole, Georgetown	37

Austin Limestone

Bucket Cave	43
Bull Creek	49
Mount Bonnell	54

Frank's Meat Market   56
Bouldering — Seider Creek   57
Bouldering — Gooch Traverse   57
University of Texas   58
Bouldering — Tenth Street   59
Bouldering — Mosquito Bridge   59
Bouldering — Sunken Gardens   60
Barton Springs Area   62
Campbell's Hole   64
New Wall   65
Gus Fruh   67
Urban Assault   71
Reimer's Fishing Ranch   77
Pace Bend Park   91

San Antonio Limestone

Guadalupe Limestone   95
Medina   100
Cub Cave   102
Metropolitan   103

Pecos Limestone
Top Secret: Sitting Bull Falls, N.M.   **118**

Leads By Grade   119
Addendum to Reimer's   139

Texas Limestone

Introduction

I started climbing because of a guidebook. One day in the fourth grade, while searching through my library's sports section, looking for book report material, I happened across an early guidebook to rockclimbing in Joshua Tree, California. What it was doing in my elementary school library in Plano, Texas, hidden amid the biographies of Bob Cousy, Vince Lombardy and Jim Thorpe, I'll never know. I do know that it altered the course of my life.

I saw immediately that rockclimbing wasn't like ordinary sports. I seem to remember that the first section of the guide was filled with accounts of near-death falls and terrible hangovers (or was it overhangs? Both, I think.) A bar, the Boom Boom Room in Twenty Nine Palms, figured prominently. There was even an outrageous essay on bouldering by someone named John Long. In short, it was more than a guidebook.

Recently, it seems, the trend in guidebooks has gone in the opposite direction. Here's the name of the route. Here's a drawing of the route. Climb it.

I like to keep up with the new trends, both in climbing and in writing. But I also remember the old style with a certain fondness. Running it out. Bolting on lead. All that macho stuff.

You can bet I don't climb that way anymore. But if the old style, as epitomized by that boisterous Joshua Tree guide creeps into my writing, skim along. I've tried to report only the facts.

Geology / History

The Cretaceous epoc was a sweet time to be alive in Texas. A warm, shallow sea covered the earth. The previous millinium had been a hot one and the ice caps melted down like sweat off a bald man's head. The influx of water raised the seas and transformed Texas into a giant hot tub of organic activity. Zillions of microscopic life forms, planktons and algaes, ancestors of the aquarium monkeys advertised on the back cover of comic books, floated through the green water like sand raised in the tides. Periodically, mammoth shoal whales swam through in herds devouring sea monkeys by the ton. Then they shat sea monkeys by the ton. Sea monkeys died and fell to the bottom. This is called Organic Precipitation.

What it looked like after several thousand years was mud. The richest mud ever. Some of it seeped and pooled and brewed and distilled into oil. Black gold, that is. The stuff that made cowboys into fools. Another story entirely.

We're concerned with the other mud. The mud that hosted the calcite producing organisms (tiny snails that secreted limestone), the reef builders, giant centipedes and carnivorous, burrowing worms. These are the organisms that built our cliffs. The hard, gray patina on much of our best limestone was produced by a limestone excreting animal. Many of the holds resulted from the activity of live organisms on the slowly solidifying mud. The deep round pockets that weave through the stone at Bucket Cave and Reimer's Ranch for example, are the petrified remnants of giant worm holes. This is called Karstic Limestone.

All in all, it was the best of times. Like the 1960's, things were happening in the Cretaceous. Consistent hot and muggy weather. Perpetual summer. Zero hour work week. Cross species sex. A crazy rate of genetic mutation. The world was your oyster bed.

Like most good women, one day, for no reason, Mother Earth grew cold. The oceans froze at the poles drawing water off of the lands. The great Cretaceous sea receeded. The sea monkeys were swept out with the tide. The aquatic worms and centipedes slithered out of their homes and followed the water to Galveston, leaving steep cliffs all over the place.

Later . . .

A few thousand years after the last centipede crawled down the beach, Homo Sapiens like you and I discovered the cliffs. Tonkawas and Comanche camped under the radical overhangs and eyed tempting climbs. Virgin lines of pockets and huecos invited bouldering and it is safe to assume that the Texas Indians, always game for tests of courage and daring, were climbers.

It is a little known but well established fact that Texas cowboys were adept at toeing pockets and dangling from heel hooks. Rope work, honed on the rock, translated easily to the ranch in the form of the lasso. The invention of a tight fitting, pointy-toed boot resulted from a desire for an effective limestone bouldering shoe. Sticky rubber came along later as the Spanish conquistadores returned from their New World road trips hooked on Texas rock.

With typical western reticence, the Texans kept their cliffs to themselves, pretending instead to be engaged in rodeo functions, 4F, Bar B. Q. and local politics. They were, in fact, cranking hard routes.

Father Clem, Keith Guillory, Goomba John and James Crump . . .

In 1970, limestone climbing at the Axis Mundi (Austin), began in earnest when Father Clem, an instructor at St. Edwards University, took a group of Whole Earth Employees to Campbell's Hole and demonstrated rockclimbing protection techniques. At roughly the same time, Lehman Holden was teaching climbing classes for the Sierra Club. Whether the two maestros ever met and joined forces for assaults on the more precipitous cliffs nearby is a matter of some speculation. We can only assume that they did.

In 1973, Keith Guillory, young and foolish and armed with a fresh pair of French varappes (slick-soled climbing shoes), began climbing the steeper faces around Campbell's Hole. This kind of hare-brained activity attracted the interest of others and soon an Austin coterie formed.

Bill Gooch became a limestone bouldering aficionado making ropeless ascents of such intimidating problems as the Zilker Soccer Field Boulder 5.10 and Slubberdegullion 5.10 on the right side of the right arch at the Waller Creek bridge.

In about 1978 Goomba John Sanders and Lauren Clayton discovered the Gus Fruh Wall and ascended Biner Talk, later known as Thumb Dance 5.10, wisely traversing right to avoid the detached flake that is now the standard exit. They also authored a 5.9 just to the left of Biner Talk known as Pussy Puss and all of the climbs on the Guide's Wall.

Goomba John was quite possibly the first non-insect to traverse the walls at Sunken Gardens despite ridicule from his peers who dismissed the area as too short. Goomba John has the last laugh, however, since Sunken Gardens has become the most popular bouldering spot in Austin.

In the early 1970's, Garth McGee and James Crump planted the seedlings of a slight rivalry on the cliffs around Campbell's Hole when James succeeded on one of Garth's projects. In contrast to present day climbing rivalries, no punches were thrown. Wild histrionics did not ensue. Soon after this, however, the Crumpian Era began.

Gifted with a wild ape index (James' arms are seven inches longer than he is tall), Crump launched a limestone carreer that included the first ascents of the Walter Weed Shuffle V5 at Bull Creek Park and Bay of Pigs 5.12d in 1983 at Thurman cove.

Sprouting bolts . . .

With the closure of Enchanted Rock in 1983, bolts began to sprout on the limestone around Austin and route development has accelerated ever since.

Scott Harris, Dave Cardosa, Hank Caylor and Greg Brooks provided Austin with it's first sport climbing wall when they uncovered and prepared The New Wall. With it's copius bolts, safe anchors and steep angle, this is the best, pure sport wall on the Greenbelt.

Scott and Jean Hudson deserve mention for their early work at Reimer's Ranch, the limestone klettergarten off the Pedernales.

Dallas area climbers are indebted to Paul Clark, Russell and Karen Rand, Jack Mileski and Duane Raleigh who collectively dropkicked standards to a new level with their ascents on the limestone at Cleburn, Texas. In fact, it has been Jack Mileski who, through his devotion to training and hardcore example, has had the single most motivating influence on limestone rock climbing in Central Texas in recent years. As his first ascents at Cleburn and Miller Springs indicate, Jack is a rock climber of the first order. But more than that, Jack is a positive force that helps to energize the people around him. Whether it is teaching English at an inner city high school in Dallas or hanging on his wrists in a sharp limestone hueco, his ethic of "Never Say Take," has spurred climbers to push their personal limits throughout the region.

In San Antonio, people like Alex Catlin, Liz Culbertson, Jacob Valdez and Joe Lowe have carried the torch of route development along the Guadalupe. Mike Lewis is responsible for ferreting out in-town climbing areas. Recently, Mike Klein, Paul Erbe, Scott Hinton and Jeb Vetter have been tearing up Cub Cave with first ascents and it is only a matter of time before new limestone areas are discovered and developed around old San Antone.

Finally, thanks goes out to John Gogas, Carrol Spoerl, Mike Lewis, Jacob Valdez, David McArthur and Alex Catlin for turning me on to their beautiful routes off the Pecos River down south.

With the adoption of such tactics as rappel bolting and the use of electric drills which expediate the development of crags exponentially, a premium must be placed on judgment. Please respect the stone. Think before putting up a new climb. Just as a piece of art reflects on its creator, a climb reflects on its first ascentionist. You will be remembered by your work. Our thanks goes out to those early first ascentionists on whose routes we learned to climb.

"The phobia concerning bolts is almost comparable to the Puritan's aversion to and fear of sex. Puritan's apparently beleived that sexual activity was not only very bad but also likely to become very popular!... To be sure, the worst fears of the Puritan's have been realized, while those of the climbing ethicists have not. Why? Maybe it's just that screwing is more enjoyable than drilling bolt holes."

— Warren "Batso" Harding, *Downward Bound*

Ethics

Traditionally, ethical debates in Central Texas have been resolved through knife fights. The combatants, armed with cleavers, grip one end of a leather belt with their teeth and circle, looking for openings. It is a strange and bloody dance, but it keeps squabbling to a minimum. Ethics vary from area to area. While locals in one area might tolerate bolting on rappel, for example, locals in another area might not. Check around before engaging in questionable tactics or carry a side-arm.

or carry a side-arm.

Access

We have chosen to include all climbing areas regardless of access problems in hopes that by publishing the abundance of restricted climbing we will prompt climbing clubs, organizations and individuals to take action.

"How can you buy or sell the sky, the warmth of the land? The idea is strange to us. If we do not own the freshness of the air and the sparkle of the water, how can you buy this?"

Dwamish Chief Sealth

NOTE: All areas with restricted access will be clearly labeled as CLOSED in the text. We will not be including directions to cliffs with restricted access. Please do not trespass on privately owned property. Trespassing is against the law.

Any access problems are indicated in the text.

Write or call your congressman, the Access Fund and local climbing club now and ask them to help us open our cliffs. Get involved.

Ratings

About a year ago, I was hired by the City of Austin to assess the climbability of a lighting structure known as the Moontower. Apparently, a drunken young man climbed up the thing and grabbed the humming wires. Zap. He fell dead.

Anyway, I visited the site with Fred Hawkins, the city attorney, climbed to the scaffolding and pronounced it 5.9.

"5.9?" Fred asked, "What the hell is that?"

Good question.

Roped climbs in this guide have been rated according to the Yosemite Decimal System, an offshoot of the 1920 German Welzennbach System which rated climbs from Class 1 (hiking) to Class 5 (roped climbing). In the 1950's, at Tahquitz Rock, Royal Robbins and the boys added the decimal to class 5 and subdivided it from 5.0 to 5.9. This worked fine until someone climbed a piece of stone that clearly outstripped the system. 5.10 was introduced as the ultimate climb. Then someone ascended a climb that was clearly harder than 5.10. American climbers resisted simply allowing the scale to expand. Rather than losing the elegant ending point of 5.10, Henry Weaselman, a little known cobbler from Peoria, Illinois, suggested subdividing 5.10 into 5.10a and 5.10b. Shortly thereafter, Gary Pokipsee ascended a 5.10c. Then 5.10d fell and everybody felt that 5.10 had had its day in the sun and the next grade appended to a modern desperate was 5.11a. 5.11b, c, and d followed, then, chaos . . . .

The trend in recent years has been to ignore the evolution of grading. The a, b, c and d subdivision within grades is now treated as shading rather than as clearly delineated jumps in difficulty. Originally, the difference between a 5.11a and a 5.11b was equal to the difference between a 5.7 and a 5.8. This softening within the grades has resulted in a spate of over-rating, chest beating and swollen egos. In an effort to check the wave, we have elected to abandon the Weaselman System of a, b, c, d in favor of the flat grade, 5.10 for example. The upper and lower regions of a grade will be indicated with a + (5.10+) or a - (5.10 -).

Rock climbing grades are largely subjective. It is your right as an

American to disagree with the rating of a particular climb or boulder problem. All complaints should be addressed to:

> The President of the United States
> District of Columbia, U. S. A.

Bouldering

Texas has an abundance of good bouldering. For this guide, the authors have chosen to adopt the Vermin rating scale, a system devised by John Sherman for rating bouldering difficulty at the Hueco Tanks. This open-ended grading system has caught on around the United States and currently extends from V0 to V12 or 13. This system takes a little getting used to, but concensus seems to indicate that V0 is roughly 5.9 or 5.10 while V7 is equivalent to a low end 5.13.

Quality Ratings

A crown (♛) indicates either a high quality climb or a route first ascended by one of the authors.

Axis Mundi

Most religions have concepts of the center of the world. The center of the world for most Catholics is the Vatican. Mecca is the Axis Mundi for many Muslims. The navel of the Buddha is the center of the world for some people. Austin, Texas is the Axis Mundi for Texas Limestone.

Accordingly, climbing areas will be described with Austin acting as a center point and Town Lake acting as the center of Austin.

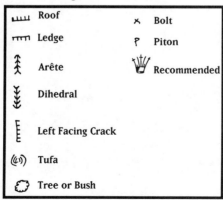

⊔⊔⊔ Roof	✗ Bolt
⊓⊓⊓ Ledge	₽ Piton
⚡ Arête	♛ Recommended
⚡ Dihedral	
⌶ Left Facing Crack	
⟮⫯⟯ Tufa	
⬭ Tree or Bush	

TOPO KEY

Jimmy Menendez, V7

Dallas Rock

Some of the best limestone climbing in America lies within two hours of Dallas, Texas at the Chisholm Wall. Unfortunately, the area is on private land and the owner has chosen to prohibit climbing. *C'est la vie.*

• *Point of Interest::* It's worth the drive to Elgin to sample Southside Meat Market's World Famous Hot Gut sausage. From Dallas, take I 35 south. Drive approximately 200 miles to highway 290. Turn left on 290 and head to Elgin. Southside Meat Market is located on the right as you enter Elgin, Texas. A perfect order consists of one pound of hot gut per person, one jalapeno, five slices of light bread, and a wedge of onion. A Blue Bell ice cream gas cap is recomended to staunch possible eruptions. Be sure to weigh in and out at the scale by the exit.

For those unable to road trip to Elgin, we've included some Dallas bistros:

• *Mexican:* Good and Cheap- Two Pesos at 1827 Greenville Ave., 267-7704. Mi Cocina, 11661 Preston Road, 265-7704.

• *Breakfast and Late Night:* Lakewood Cafe, 2111 Abrams , 823-0313 for night owls. Open till 4 a.m.

• *Coffee:* Clover Restaurant, 233 Continental, 742-3321

•*Beer:* Rattlesnake

• *Vegetarian:* Dream Cafe 2800 Routh St. 954-0486 for the hardcore vegie bowel wrap. Whole Foods, 2218 Greenville Ave., 824-1744.

• *Carnivore:* Angelo's B. B. Q. (Ft. Worth) Open 11am to 10 pm. Closed Sunday. Cold beer on tap. 2533 White Settlement, 332-0357.

• *Groceries:* Whole Foods, 2218 Greenville Ave., 824-1744.

• *Massage/Rolfing:* Whole Foods

• *Gear:* Mountian Hideout 14010 Coit Road 234-8651, Whole Earth 5400 E. Mockingbird, 824-7444, Mountain Sports 2025 W Pioneer Pkwy in Arlington, 461-4503.

• *Camping:* Mineral Wells State Park offers camping. Camping is allowed around most area lakes.

PLANO PYRAMIDS — BOULDERING

Directions: From Austin, take I35 North to 75 North (Central Expressway). 75 North through Plano to the Spring Creek Exit. Drive down the access road past Spring Creek and park at the dirt road on the right that leads between two pyramid-shaped concrete buttresses. The buttress on the right is split by Snake Crack V1. Apis Bull V3 is found on the right wall below the railroad tracks. To reach the good bouldering/climbing on the Obelisk, walk north down the tracks and look for the tall, freestanding concrete pillar on the left.

General Description: Railroad trestle. Abandonded highway buttress. Manufactured climbing on good cement.

First Trestle
1. Snake Crack V2 ₩
2. Apis Bull V3

The Obelisk
(right to left)
3. See You in Nogales V3 ₩
4. Back to School V2
5. Crabs V2 ₩
6. Disney Fignus 5.12- (bolts) ₩ Jeff Jackson

RENNER ROAD — BOULDERING

Directions: From Austin, take I 35 North to 75 North. Take 75 north through Dallas to Richardson (about twenty minutes). Exit Renner Road and turn right. Turn right again into the office building parking lot before crossing the railroad tracks. Park at the southeast corner and follow a trail downhill to the railroad trestle.

General Description: Railroad trestle. Flagstone traverse. Cement slab. Cement pillars. This area offers good all around training possibilities from V1 smearing to V7 edges. Note: For a few days every winter, good, scary ice conditions exist on the shale cliffs that parallel the creek under the trestle. The most infamous line, Real Short Eiger, can be found by continuing along Renner Road over the railroad tracks and turning right on Highway 5 (Spring Creek Road). Drive along this road until you reach the bridge that crosses Spring Creek. Real Short Eiger is the steep, shale wall on the right that looks like it might just be climbable if the ice holds.

Slab (across the creek from the flagstone pillar)
left to right
1. Corner V1
2. Rust Streak V2
3. Middle Route V2 ♛
4. Razor's Edge V2 ♛ Finish by climbing the underside of the iron girder to the flagstone pillar for a pumpy, seventy foot roof. 5.10 F.A. Keith Wright
5. Pockets V2
6. Bolt Route V2 (Ascend the slab using only the protruding rebar stems.)
(A V0 glue-on route now exists between Pockets and the Bolt Route.)

Jungle Buttress (in the trees west of the slab)
left to right
7. Yoga Corner V2 ♛
8. Jane V2
9. Cheeta V2
10. Tantor V2
11. Tarzan V6 ♛

Pillar (flagstone pillar)
Traverse the Pillar staying below the capstone for a V3 pump.
12. Super Lunge V5 ♛ (From the inch wide ledge, dyno to the top of the girder).

13. Many V2 problems and variants exist

Zulu Buttress (in the trees west of the pillar)

Starting on the south face, right to left . . .

14. Ant Farm V6
15. Crom's Hoary Beard V3
16. Shaka Khan V5
17. Shaka Zulu V5 ₩ (last problem on the south face)
18. V4
19. V3
20. Canary V2 ₩
21. Hooks V7/8 (shallow mono-doigts)
22. V2
23. V3

MATILDA BRIDGE — BOULDERING

Directions: Central (75) north to Mockingbird exit. Turn Right. Left on Matilda. Pull off to the left on the first concrete drive. Jump the curb and follow the dirt road under the bridge. Climbing is on the far side of the bridge.

General Description: Vertical glue-on traverses. Two cracks. Three up routes.

1. Camel Crack 5.9 (Crack on the far right.)
2. 5.10+ (Glue-on just to the left of Camel.)
3. 5.11- (Glue-on to the left.)
4. Double Smuggled Tamales 5.12+ Ty Foose (One bolt. Chipped route up the third full panel to the right. First Ascent soloed.)
5. Thin Crack 5.12 (Thin crack at the left end of glue-on traverse.)

TRAMMEL TRESTLE — BOULDERING

Directions: I35 North to 75 North. Exit Mockingbird and turn right. Mockingbird (3 miles) to Rockaway. Left on Rockaway to Fisher. Turn Left. Cross railroad tracks and park at the tennis courts on the left. Climbs are under the railroad trestle.

General Description: Cement pockets and edges. Track Crack 5.7. Great training for limestone pocket climbing. High bouldering. Bolts for toproping. All climbs were first soloed by Jack Mileski.

1. Conquer'ete 5.11
2. Track Crack 5.7 ᵂ
3. Du Dihedral 5.10
4. Jesus Rules 5.11 ᵂ
5. Super Pro 5.10
6. Stylin' 5.10 ᵂ
7. Aid Crack
8. Arc de Triomphe 5.12- ᵂ
9. ?
10. ?
11. Dark Man 5.9 ᵂ
12. Blade Pull A V2
13. Blade Pull B V2
14. Blade Pull C V2
15. Epoxy Hair Care V1
16. Another Blade Pull

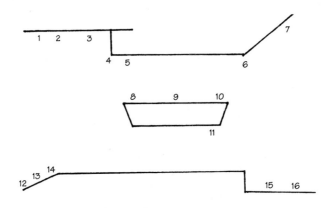

TRAMMEL TRESTLE

TIETZE PARK — BOULDERING

Directions: Mockingbird to Skillman. Turn Right. Skillman to Vanderbuilt. Park at Park!

General Description: Flagstone buildering. High Traverse 5.12. Low Traverse 5.11.

MALONE WALL — BOULDERING

Traverse the limestone cliff on the north side of Harry Hines at the Tollway by the City Mark Office Complex.

LAKE MINERAL WELLS

Directions: I35 North to 35 West towards Ft. Worth. 180 West to Mineral Wells. About one mile before the city of Mineral Wells, look for a sign on the right "Mineral Wells State Park." Technical climbers must register at the Park Headquarters. Follow signs to the climbing.

General Description: Mineral Wells is a State Park that allows toprope climbing only. The climbing area, known as Penitentiary Hollow, consists of a maze-like collection of short sandstone conglomerate cliffs which offer an abundance of technical challenges for the moderate climber. Climbing in the Main Canyon involves wild pebble pinches and balancey face moves while the side canyons offer overhanging jugs and pockets. (No first ascents will be listed for top rope climbs.)

The Refrigerator

1. Offwidth Lieback 5.8
2. Arrow Flake 5.8
3. Arete 5.10
4. Dave's Boulder Problem 5.8
5. Miscellaneous B. P. Traverse 5.?
6. George Hazzard Route 5.8

Scenic Overlook

7. Practice Wall 5.7-5.9
8. Big Offwidth 5.5
9. Short Routes 5.6

Main Canyon (left)

10. 5.8 Boulder Problem
11. Another Dave Problem (tree) 5.8
12. Short Easy Crack 5.7

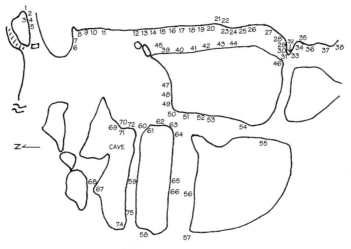

MINERAL WELLS

13. Slap Roof 5.8
14. Alaskan Crack 5.5
15. Finger Stinger 5.11- ☙
16. Thin Crack 5.10
17. Bestard Climb 5.10
18. 5.10 Layback
19. Heat Seeker 5.11-
20. Hand Crack 5.7
21. Apples to Hell 5.10
22. Oz 5.11

23. The Short Unnamed 5.10
24. Hand Crack 5.7+
25. Something in Between 5.10
26. Two Fingers Tequilla 5.10
27. Moderate to Easy
28. Easy Tower 5.5
29. Unfinished Experiment V?
30. One Weird V2
31. Another Weird V3
32. Downclimb 5.2

Big Overhang
33. Crumbly 5.9
34. Trash Crack 5.5
35. Thieves and Assholes 5.10+
36. Hidden Jewel 5.11
37. Keith's Way 5.11
38. Gandolf 5.11+

Main Canyon (right)
39. Rewritten 5.7
40. Connect the Pockets 5.9
41. In Search of Green 5.8
42. Green Variation 5.9+
43. Roof Right of Mulberry 5.7
44. Line Left of Mulberry 5.7
45. Traverse from Mulberry 5.?
46. Big Boulder Traverse 5.?

Backside of Main Canyon
47. Black Flag 5.10
48. Easy Face 5.6

49. Finger Crack 5.8
50. Vacation 5.11b
51. Immigrant 5.11
52. Right of Immigrant 5.10
53. Under Immigrant 5.10
54. Sandstone Roof 5.?
55. Break Rock (4 Problems 5.7-5.9)

Side Canyons

56. Boulder Wall 5.4-5.5
57. 5.9 Roof Routes
58. Dynamo Hum 5.11
59. Easy Wall 5.5-5.7
60. Arete Solo 5.6
61. Hilo Traverse 5.8
62. Solo Crack 5.7
63. Grey Streak 5.?
64. Downhill Crack Traverse 5.9
65. Easy Crack 5.6
66. Sandstone Roof 5.8+
67. Pee Wee's 5.10 ♔
68. Line Left 5.10

First Overhang

69. B. P. Traverse 5.6
70. 5.9 Variation
71. 5.8 Overhang
72. Easy Face 5.8
73. Easy Routes 5.5-5.7
74. Uphill Traverse 5.9+
75. Beastie Boys 5.?
. . . and various other boulder problems

"The white man," as one indian said, "was in the Black Hills just like maggots," wasicu, or "the greedy one" (literally, "he-who-takes-the-fat"), was the term the Lakota used to describe the miners, and it later became their term for whites in general. "The love of possessions is a disease with them," said Sitting Bull, who was never behindhand in his contempt.
— Peter Matthiessen, *In The Spirit of Crazy Horse*

Fred Mitchel, *Mainstay* 12+   Photo by Jack Mileski

Cleburn, Texas / The Chisholm Wall

CLOSED

Directions: CLOSED. SEE ACCESS.

Access: For several years now a gun-toting friend of the landowner has patrolled the cliff. He insists that there is NO ROCKCLIMBING ALLOWED.

General Description: The Burn, with it's smooth gray bellies and numerous pockets, was the original hardcore Texas limestone climbing area. Henry Barber, a well known East Coast climber, called it the best limestone area in America. Henry's declaration is a bit inflated but the Burn really is a pretty darn good cliff.

The Burn

1. Various boulder problems (A steep trail cuts uphill just after the fence crossing. Take this to the base of the cliffs and turn left. A trail runs the length of the cliff. Climbs are listed right to left.)

Short Wall

(This is the first 20' wall, characterized by green lichen.)

2. Right Wall 5.7
3. Green Dihedral 5.5
4. Tricam Crack 5.7

Mr. Cricket Area

(Black wall characterized by an acute corner. The left wall is cut by a right tending crack with a pin.)

5. Mr. Cricket Goes to Washington 5.8 A3 (Nail the seam out a roof on the wall right of the corner and climb the wide crack above.)
6. Mr. Cricket 5.6 (Stem the dihedral.)
7. Sweet Dreams 5.10 (Toprope the black face starting right of the thin crack.)
8. Bad Dreams 5.9+ ♛ (Thin crack with a pin.)

Dutchman Area

(Characterized by a huge, bell shaped roof.)

9. Omen 5.12 (Steep, bolted climb right of the roof.)

10. The Flying Dutchman 5.10+ ♛ (Climb through the bell shaped roof. 2 bolts.)

Planet X

(Characterized by 30' roofs pocked with body sized huecos.)

11. King Jug 5.10 (The first bolted route right of the roofs.)

12. Armageddon 5.10

13. Blatty Crack 5.11- (Crack with a drilled angle.)

14. Wild Planet 5.11+ ♛ (Starts in Planet X crack moves right to finish.)

15. Planet X 5.10 ♛♛ (Climb the 30' roof crack. Tricky pro.)

16. Romulus 5.13- (Bolts left of Planet X.)

17. Remus 5.13 ♛ (Left of Romulus.)

18. Serpent and the Rainbow 5.12 ♛ (Climb into the huge hueco and exit right.)

19. Pocket Pussy 5.12- (Look for the bolt 100' left of Serpent. Bring pro for the exit crack.)

Overlooked Wall

(Vertical wall with several bolted lines.)

20. Strategic Arms 5.10-

21. Texas Constitution 5.8 (Crack/seam to roof. Orange/yellow lichen. 5.11 variation goes left at roof.)

22. The French Connection 5.11+ ♛ (Balancey face.)

23. Magic Carpet Ride 5.10- ♛♛ (Hard to protect seam.)

24. Snake Eyes 5.10

25. Constellation Bear 5.8 (Ramp)

26. Frog Dance 5.11- (Climbs the face after the wall bends left.)

27. Agent Orange 5.9 (Top rope the heavily pocketed wall down the trail from the Overlooked Wall. Characterized by orange lichen.)

28. Monkey Shines 5.12- ♛ (Monkey right out a shelf and climb the overhanging wall above. Look for the old black thread.)

Prow Area
(Characterized by steep slabs and an area of wall that has collapsed and formed a section of distinctive, though rotten, yellow rock. This section is known as The Break.)
29. Josh's 11 (This is the first bolted route after passing under the giant roofs. Slab.)
30. Lust for Life 5.12 ♛
31. Hieroglyphics 5.13
32. The Decimator 5.12- ♛
33. The Minotaur 5.12+ ♛♛ (Climbs the obvious prow.)
34. Rodeo on the Brazos 5.12 (Starts Scarface and moves right.)
35. Scarface 5.12- (Bolts left of the prow.)
36. Moody Blues 5.10 (Start at good holds and pull onto slab)
37. Trouble in River City 5.9X (Start left of Moody and climb slab.)
38. Skeksis II 5.9 (Right crack.)
39. Skeksis I 5.7 (Left crack.)
40. Funky Comadina 5.11+ (Bolts left of Skeksis.)
41. Painted Bird 5.12
42. Drunken Boat 5.12
The following climbs are located left of The Break.
43. Cyclops 5.11 ♛ (The obvious white prow.)
44. Dirty Legs 5.11 (Toprope the easy looking dihedral 200 yards left of Cyclops.)
45. Tai Chi 5.10 (This high boulder problem climbs a crack 100 yards left of Dirty.)

Calcutta
(Identified by the large boulders that block the trail.)
46. Willingjam 5.11 (Toprope through the huge hueco.)

47. Calcutta Bunghole 5.12 (Toprope through the series of fins and
knobs.)

48. Diagonal 5.4

Indian Staircase

(Look for the polished access to the top of the cliffs.)

49. Project Dog 5.12+ (Toprope through the concave face right of the
Flakes.)

50. Gelfling Flakes 5.11 (Bolts angle left.)

51. Squaw Creek 5.9 (Tricams in pockets protect this climb on the right
face of Kurt's Crack.)

52. Kurt's Crack 5.7 ☖

53. Sundance 5.10 (Climb the face left of Kurt's.)

54. Pegboard 5.10 (Left of Sundance.)

55. Indian Staircase Crack 5.6 ☖

56. Wedding Bells 5.10- ☖ (Bolt left of the staircase.)

57. Love on the Rocks 5.10+ ☖

58. Force of One 5.11 (Pull roof by bolts.)

59. Fatal Attraction 5.10+ (Climb seam.)

60. War of the Worlds 5.12- ☖ (Climb to hueco and straight out.)

61. Blitzkrieg 5.12 ☖

62. The Drone 5.12 ☖

Lizard Wall

(Characterized by green lichen and a huge roof on it's right side.)

63. Bone Sheath 5.12+ (Climbs through the left side of the roof.)

64. Blue Velvet 5.12 ☖

65. Gila Mama 5.10+ ☖ (Boulder to the hueco and clip a hidden, fixed
pin. Bring pro. for the exit crack.)

66. Hopi Snake Dance 5.11 ☖ (Move left through huecos.)

67. Lizard King 5.13-

68. Gecko Man 5.11- ☖

69. The Obsession 5.11 ♛♛ (Climb to the obvious hueco and out.)

70. Hey Zeus 5.12- ♛

71. Dino 5.10 (Toprope the face where the wall bends left.)

72. Such a Flake 5.7

Gay Bar

(Starts at the thick cedar tree)

73. Turn of the Screw 5.12- (Stick clip a high bolt and lunge to a hueco.)

74. Johnny Law 5.11 ♛♛ (Follow bolts right.)

75. One Adam Twelve 5.12 (Follow good holds to a heinous exit.)

76. Deputy Dog 5.10 (Bolts move left.)

77. Gay Bar Problem 5.10+ ♛ (Very committing boulder problem just right of a green dihedral.)

78. Gay Bar Crack 5.6 (Dihedral.)

High Seas

(Characterized by a steep drop downhill on the trail that leads to a very steep wall. Linda Blair and Cactus Jack are located before the drop. The other climbs are accessible by climbing onto the shelf before or after the downhill.)

79. Linda Blair 5.10 A1 (Climb the wide crack.)

80. Cactus Jack 5.10+ ♛ (Toprope the face left of Linda.)

The following climbs begin on the right side of the upper shelf.

81. Black Rain 5.12- ♛ (High stick clip.)

82. The Albatross 5.13

83. Aqualung 5.12- ♛

84. Archetype 5.12 ♛

85. Mainstay 5.12+ ♛

86. Mariner 5.13- ♛♛ (Ultra-classic pocket crack.)

87. The Insulter 5.13 ♛

88. Monogun 5.13- ♛

The Amphitheater

(Around the corner from the High Seas)

89. Pocket Crack A3

Kryptonite

(The next section of tall walls past the Amphitheater.)

90. Karen's Crack 5.7
91. The Sorcerer 5.11 (Climb the seam and move left onto a face by a bolt.)
92. New Chipped Route 5.12-
93. Kryptonite 5.11 ☙ (Around the corner from the New Chipped Route you'll find this classic roof crack.)

"I didn't come to the mountains or choose to live in the mountains just to run into some new code of conformity, rules, and regulations. If there are those that find it necessary and desirable to institutionalize climbing, fine with me. I'm quite satisfied with what I've been doing and will continue to do so."

— Warren Harding, Downward Bound

Ze Nono Gunner! Mal hombre
es muy desperado...!

Houston Rock?

This just in from the concrete jungle:

"As the sun drops over the horizon, and the pink and yellow turn to a darker blue, I watch the outline of the pine forests turn black as night. The lights from Houston keep that outline visible the entire night.

"Sometimes, late, as I drive home from my job, I ponder the forest's resemblance to the Texas Hill Country when the lights from Austin keep the hills visible at night. I think I long for those hills most at that moment. Why? Not for their sheer and serene beauty, and not for their cedar trees and perfect seasons, and not even because of the good times around a cedar fire on a near perfect camping trip. I long for the hills and their limestone which in the past has provided me with some ideal sport climbing.

"The fact that Austin is three hours away for those of us that obey traffic laws has left many Houston climbers frustrated, but the frustration can be lessened. Many buildings in the Houston area are built with limestone from Hill Country quarries.

"Buildering is not admired by peace officers and building owners and I have been thrown off of routes by both and told never to come back. But late at night the buildings are closed and the officers are at Shipley's Donuts. The following buildering spots around Houston are definitely off limits."

Andy Klier — Houstonian At Large

Champions Place

Directions: From Downtown Houston take I 45 North to FM 1960. Follow 1960w all the way to Champions Rd. (If you see the mall, you've gone too far.) Turn right on Champions and take your first left into the shopping center. Park at the cleaners.

1. Is That a Spider B5.11- (Looking at the pay phone by the convenience store, walk left and around a corner. Start 3 ft. from the corner. Traverse right, up and to the monodoight.)
2. Godzilla B5.9 (Starts around corner from Spider on the huge ledge. Move up and right to the mono.)
3. Pregnant Catfish B5.8 (Wall between the convenience store and cleaners. Up the left corner.)
4. IBC Rules B5.10 (Start on the sidepull just right of Catfish. Climb to the top and traverse left.)
5. Toad B5.7 (Start right of payphone and climb to the roof of the convenience store.)

Pooch and Ellie's Wall

(This wall is found in the same parking lot as Champions Place, further down 1960 at the Italian Restaurant.)

1. Green Green Rocky Road 5.8 (This two and a half story slab is located in back and farthest away from the entrance.)
2. My House From Here 5.8 (Same slab closest to the entrance.)

V Hex

Directions: From downtown take 610 to 290 west and exit Barker Cypress. Take a left on Barker Cypress (over 290). Take the next left and park at a bridge covered in hexagonal blocks.

De Seis Tiros B5.10 (Traverse the wall.)

Stone Gate Subdivision

Directions: From downtown take I45 North to FM 1960 West. Go west on 1960 all the way to Champions Forest. Take a right on Champions Forest and drive to Cypresswood. Park at the Kroger at that corner and walk across Cypresswood.

1. Traverse the 200', crimpy wall. B5.10

Albury Wall

Directions: From downtown take I 45 North to 249 North towards Tomball.
Follow 249 almost to Tomball, and turn right on Holderith Rd. Drive
Holderith until the road deadends into Huffsmith Koreville. Look for the big
gates of Albury Manor. Park where you can and walk to the entrance of this
subdivision. The routes are located on the back side of the brick wall to your
right.

1. Almost Better Than Sex B5.12- Start at the end of the huge, welded
   bar at the chiseled holes and traverse left.
2. Duck Face B5.9 This cool problem starts at the far right with hands
   matched in the giant hole. The top is not on until you get to the top
   of the brick pillar.
3. Santa's Helper B5.8 Chimney just right of Sex.
4. Bricks are for Kids B5.8 This fun layback is found on the front side of
   the left wall on the tallest pillar. The light is off route.

Many more possibilities exist here.

_____

"Never is force opposed with force; instead it is overcome with yeilding."

— Benjamin Hoff, *The Tao of Pooh*

_____

Adrian Harris, *Desert Storm* 5.13+   Photo by Jack Mileski

Temple / Belton Limestone

Basics:
* *Food:* Both Temple and Belton offer a variety of restaurants. A grocery store (HEB) is located in Belton about a mile from the cliffs.
* *Camping:* Camping is allowed at Temple Lake Park approximately three miles from the cliffs. Do not camp at the crag.

MILLER SPRINGS (AKA TEMPLE/BELTON)

Directions: From Austin, take I35 North to Belton (69 miles). Get off at exit 293A and turn left at the stop sign. Turn right onto Main (317) and drive through Belton. Take a left onto 439 and then turn right onto 2271 and follow this to a parking area on the north side of the dam. Park here and walk east across an open field to a good trail. Follow the trail downhill to a dirt road which leads to the cliffs.

General Description: These beautiful, overhanging cliffs offer difficult and gymnastic sport climbs. A premium is placed on meat pulling. A strong back is a prerequisite for success here.

Access: The cliffs at Miller Springs are currently being leased by the Miller Springs Nature Alliance. Climbing is allowed **by permit only** until the Alliance completes an environmental impact study. For information concerning permits please contact Martin Tull at Mountain Hideout (214) 350-8181 or Texas Mountain Guides at (512) 482-9208. Unless you have a permit, or are the guest of a permit holder, there is **no climbing** at these cliffs.

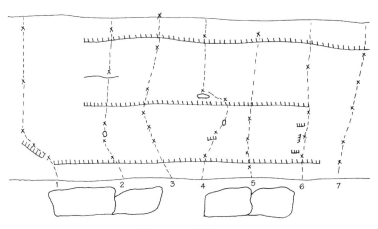

FRONT WALL

Front Wall

(left to right)

1. Misery 5.12 Russell Rand (Obvious crack to hard face moves.)
2. Concentrics 5.12 ⚜ Jack Mileski (Mono to undercling to hueco etc.)
3. Desert Shield 5.13 ⚜ Jeff Jackson (Pretty darn blank face.) Desert
   Storm 5.13+⚜⚜ (Start under the roof and climb into the Shield.
   FA Dan Durland.)
4. Raison d'etre 5.12+ ⚜ Jack Mileski (Horizontal to pockets.)
5. De La Soul 5.12+ ⚜ Jack Mileski, Jeff Jackson (45 degree gray wall.)
6. Semantics 5.12 Jeff Jackson (Corners to cap.)
7. Ass Bar 5.12- Jack Mileski (Hard start to ass bar rest. Pull roof.)
8. Primadonna 5.12 Jeff Jackson (Crack to hueco. Move left and up.)
9. Crack 5.10 Jack Mileski
10. Hippy Chick 5.10 Karen Rand (Move right out of crack.)
11. Disconnected (project)
12. Kinetics 5.12 ⚜ Paul Clark, Jack Mileski (Flake to hard roof moves.)

Paul Clark, *The Gauntlet* 5.12　　　　　　Photo by Jack Mileski

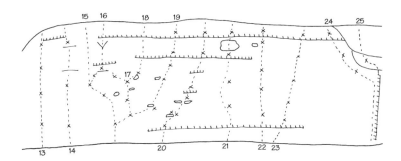

Wrath Wall

Wrath Wall (left to right)

13. Hyperactive 5.11 Russell Rand (Left hand bolt line.)

14. Pocket Envy 5.12 Jeff Jackson (Spray of pockets up white face.)

15. Cosmic Thang 5.12 Russell Rand (Start Zenith and move left at second bolt.)

16. Zenith 5.12- Paul Clark (Climb the gray streak.)

17. Steel Wheels 5.12 ♛ Jack Mileski (Climb to the orange gland, through a hueco to the South America pocket. Cut left.)

18. Gauntlet 5.12 Jack Mileski (Climb to the South America pocket and continue up.)

19. Wrath 5.13 ♛ Jack Mileski (Pull right from the orange gland on Steel Wheels into a right hand hueco. Angle right and up.)

20. Mr. Sir 5.13- ♛♛ Jack Mileski (The Classic! Climb to a butterfly-shaped hold. Lunge to the Dragonfly. Hump up and right.)

21. Septic 5.13- ♛ Jack Mileski (Climb the drips right of Sir into a Tank-sized hueco. Pull the roof.)

22. Journeyman 5.13 ♛ Jeff Jackson, Jack Mileski (Bolts right of Septic. Climb to the Vampire House and attempt to rest up for the roof above.)

23. The Chronic 5.13 ♛ Alex Catlin (Right of Journeyman)

24. Punishment (project)

25. Roofus 5.12-X Jeff Jackson, Cristina Jackson (Traverse right out the overlap to hard roof pulling.)

Morgan's Point

Directions: To climb at Morgan's Point, follow 2271 north, past a firestation and park at the Morgan's Point Community Center (at the swimming pool). Follow the pavement downhill to the edge of the lake. Scramble right along the bank to this bolted wall. Please do not top out on climbs here. There is a private residence on top of the cliff.

(Left to Right)

0. 12+ Clayton R.
1. Mike Klein 12
2. Mikey's Warm-up 5.11- Mike Klein
3. Whitey 5.11+ Dan Durland
4. Bad Bolts 11
5. Project
6. Nubian Nation 5.11+ ♛ Jack Mileski
7. Coup D'etat 5.12 ♛ Jack Mileski
8. Anglo Saxon 5.12- ♛ Jeff Jackson, Jack Mileski
9. Lefty 5.11 Russel Rand (Power up straight from the second bolt on Anglo Saxon.)
10. Pancho 5.11 ♛ Russel Rand (Roof Problem. 4 bolts.)
11. Lackey 5.12- Jack Mileski

Georgetown
Limestone

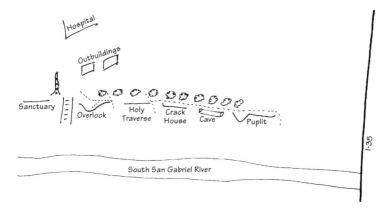

Hospital

Outbuildings

Sanctuary

Overlook   Holy   Crack   Cave   Puplit
           Traverse House

I-35

South San Gabriel River

GEORGETOWN OVERVIEW

THE RIVERSIDE SANCTUARY

Directions: From Austin, take I 35 North to Georgetown. Exit Leander (to the hospital). Take your first left, then left again into the Georgetown Hospital parking lot. Park only at the south end of the hospital parking lot near the Telesis Institute. Walk north towards a large antenae behind some outbuildings. Look for a trail, the Harpole Access, that leads downhill to the river. Thanks to Luke Stallings, Chris, Liz and the gang at the Telesis Institute for allowing climbers access to these fun bluffs.

General Description: Easy and moderate topropes with good fixed anchors. Beautiful setting.

The Sanctuary Wall

(Cut right at the split rock at the base of the Harpole Access to reach this lovely, open area. Anchors are located along the top of the cliff. Routes

described left to right as you face the cliff.)
1. Short Green Dihedral 5.8
2. Narthex 5.10 (Incipient crack to a right-facing dihedral.)
3. Angling System 5.10
4. 5.10
5. Gateway 5.10-
6. Use the Force, Luke 5.11

Sanctuary Boulders
(These problems ascend the large boulders opposite the Sanctuary Wall.)
1. Pyramid Access 5.3 (Climb either side of the pyramid-shaped dagger.)
The following problems are located on the far side of the boulders.
Toprope anchors are located on top.
2. Balcony Problems 5.6 to 5.9 (Climb the pocked face anywhere.
   Follow the crack for a nice 5.6.)
3. Above the Catacombs 5.7 (Another pocked face located over the
   boulder pile to the right of The Balcony.)

Overlook
(Go left at the base of the Harpole Access. The Overlook is the promi-
nant prow split by a crack that angles up and right over a white cave. A
large boulder leans against the base of this wall.)
1. Overlook 5.10 (Toprope the left arete and finish left or follow the crack
   right.)
2. Holy Traverse 5.7 (Follow the trail past the Overlook (west) until you
   reach a band of heavily karstic rock. Secure a line fixed between the
   bolt (backed up with the nearby tree) and the big cedar 50' to the
   right.)
3. The Crack House (Continue west to reach this rectangular cave cut by
   a seam and a crack. Toprope anchors. 5.12's live here, as do 5.9's).
4. The Pulpit 5.6 (West to the obvious, pocketed phallus. Toprope
   anchors. One of the best climbs of this grade in Central Texas.)

BLUE HOLE — BOULDERING

Directions: Drive north from Austin on I 35 for approximately thirty minutes. Get off at the Southwestern University exit. Turn Right. At Scenic Drive, turn left and follow signs to Blue Hole. Left at the graveyard takes you to the parkng area.

General Description: A classic swimming hole. Blue Hole was first described to me by Ian Powell at the 1992 Hueco Tanks Rock Rodeo. Up to thirty feet tall. Steep limestone with pockets. Deep water landings that have been well-tested by the local college population. My writing class at Southwestern University insisted that I check it out. If you like bouldering and big falls, you should check it out, too.

Starting on the slick rock at water level sometimes seems too heinous. Try downclimbing from the rim. Bring an old pair of climbing shoes.

"Elegance still demands attention but invariably runs a poor second to conquest. Lacking the formal rules of other competitive sporting events, climbing overcompensates and suffers severely through a rigid societal paradigm imposed by the contemporary climbing community. Great technical progress has been made in the last 20 years, but at the expense of creative metaphysical and spiritual diversification. Although there is substantial variety, the philosophical premises of difficulty and risk remain inviolate. The very structure of the language we use imposes conceptual barriers. Even so slight a concession as the use of terms such as '5.10,' 'XS,' or 'B1' ensnares the climber in the inflexible paradigm. There are, nevertheless, other ways to approach [climbing], ways that open the mind to aesthetic and mystical experiences and allow this unique medium to be a vehicle for reorientation with one's enviroment; ways that are inaccessible unless we intentionally avoid emersion in the strong beguiling current of the midstream with its almost irresistible inertia."
— John Gill, The Vertical Path

Marlo Mata, *Liposuction* 5.12-

Photo by J. Rebecca Gonzales

Austin Limestone

Austin, Texas is home to a variety of limestone cliffs ranging from small bouldering areas to well developed sport crags

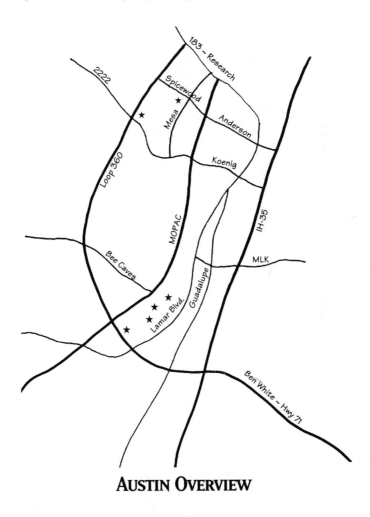

AUSTIN OVERVIEW

For those individuals unable to make the drive to Elgin's Southside Meat Market, we've included these Austin bistros.

• *Mexican:* Sunday night is Mole night at Guerro's. The only way to go for a healthy pack. Look at the ad on page 141 for the new location. Don't miss a visit to Julio's at the corner of Duval and 43rd street for a rotisserie chicken or delightful soft tacos. Other, less healthful options, include the traditional Guide hangout, Chuy's on 1728 Barton Springs Road and El Arroyo on 1624 West Fifth Street. For a Tex Mex orgasm try El Arroyo's Bar B. Q. Chicken Enchiladas with a Shiner Bock gully washer. Great deals on Happy Hour Margs.

• *Vegetarian:* Mother's at 4215 Duval, across from Julio's. Martin Bros. at 2815 Guadalupe.

• *Carnivore:* Sam's Bar B. Q. 2000 east 12th. Ribs, ribs, ribs! For full on, Hillbilly binge session and classic cowboy atmosphere, Salt Lick, Driftwood, Texas— (512) 444-8687.

• *Breakfasts and Late Night:* Try Heidi's Bakery for breakfast schneken. 2504 Lake Austin Blvd. For Late Night jam sessions Magnolia Cafe at 2304 Lake Austin Blvd. And for pancakes at all hours, Kerbey Lane Cafe at 3704 Kerbey Lane. Last minute provisions— Bagel Manufactory 2200 Guadalupe, up the street from Quack's.

• *Coffee:* For the true 'fien afficiando, Anderson's Coffee located two buildings north of Kerbey Lane offers coffee imported from everywhere and freshly roasted on Mondays and Thursdays. Try the "Pow Pow" New Guinea blend. Quackenbushes at 2120 Guadalupe is a mandatory Espresso and Cappuccino stop.

• *Beer:* Shiner Bock.

• *Groceries:* Whole Foods Market, see advertisement for locations. Also HEB Central Market 4001 N. Lamar.

• *Gear:* All the essentials can be purchased at Whole Earth Provision Company (Brodie Oaks Shopping Center) 4006 South Lamar and 2410 San Antonio Street.

A stiff toothbrush comes in handy on less traveled ground. Bring tape to protect fingers when climbing sharp pockets.

• *Camping:* The climbing areas in Austin proper do not allow camping. Here are a few options. (1) Lake Austin Metropolitan Park— 2222 to City Park

Road. Turn left and wind to the shores of Lake Austin. Plenty of camping space. (2) Camp Choutaugua (inside Pace Bend Park) Texas 71 to FM 2322. Turn right. Tent sites and electricity. Unique climbing and cliff jumping possibilities Call 264-1752 for reservation info. 3. Austin International Hostel— 2200 South Lake Shore Blvd. (512) 444-2294. (YHA affiliated).

Jeff Jackson, *Kevorkian V6*

Photo by Kevin Gallagher

Bucket Cave and the Grot

Directions: CLOSED

General Description: Without a doubt, the best bouldering in Austin. Like Hueco's Bucket Roof only much bigger.

Anthropology: At one time, Bucket Cave was inhabited by a band of Tonkawa Indians who (in accordance with those strict Sierra Club precepts— Take Only Photographs, Leave Only Footprints) left no visible trace of their passing except their bones. This is, of course, an environmentally correct impact level.

History: During prohibition, there was a sourmash still in Bucket Cave which gave the area one of its names, Stillhouse Springs.

Ecology: The springs in Bucket Cave are home to an endangered salamander.

Access: Because of the cave's ecological, anthropological and historical prominence, the ruling classes have requested that Bucket Cave remain CLOSED to the public.

The idea, most often put forward by "conservationists," that natural areas must be restricted in order to protect them has always seemed like bunk to me. Choosing to keep an in-town, natural area like Bucket Cave "closed" is like inviting the local pre-teen population to hang out, sniff glue, spray paint the walls and dig for arrowheads. In this age of industrialization, sprawling cities and rampant private ownership, free enjoyment of those few remaining natural areas should be the birthright of every Texan. We are surrounded by enough fences and guardrails.

The solution, overlooked by both the conservationists and the bureaucrats, is to allow everyone free access. Everyone. Free Access. Environmentally sensitive and anthropologically prominent areas should be marked as such, but we should not be restricted access to one of the very few remaining natural areas in Austin. The Cave has been home to people for thousands of years, people have always interacted with the cave's eco-system. Is it right to shut us out now?

Rock climbers have been recognized by park officials in many natural areas as the most environmentally conscious user group, surpassing both hikers and bikers in minimizing their impact on resources. At Miller Springs in Belton, Texas, opening the cliffs to rock climbing has eliminated the partying and spray painting that once occurred every weekend. It follows that allowing climbing in Bucket Cave would not only open another natural resource to the population of Austin, but would help protect this resource from other, less-aware user groups.

Parks Official James Crump is working towards opening the cave.

"Then suddenly he knew why he had never wanted to own any of it, arrest at least that much of what people called progress, measure his longevity at least against that much of its ultimate fate. It was because there was just exactly enough of it . . . He seemed to see the two of them – himself and the wilderness – as coevals . . . The two spans running out together, not toward oblivion, nothingness, but into a dimenson free of both time and space where once more the untreed land warped and rung to mathmatical squares of rank cotton for the frantic old-world people to turn into shells to shoot at one another, would find ample room for both-- the names the faces of the old men he had known and loved and for a little while outlived, moving again among the shades of tall, unaxed trees and sightless breaks where the wild strong immortal game ran forever before the tireless belling immortal hounds, falling and rising phoenix-like to the soundless guns."

– William Faulkner, *Go Down, Moses*

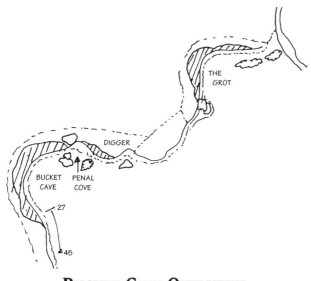

BUCKET CAVE OVERVIEW

The Grot (Right to Left)

1. Butch V1 (Starts on the right side of big boulder. Follow big holds to the top.)
2. Mount the Puppy V2 (Start off the center of boulder.)
3. Pup Left V3+ (Move left along lip of roof.)
4. Agent Orange V4 (Hard problem left of Pup.)
5. Santiago's V2 (Starts off left side of next, left boulder. Follow cool bulge to pockets.)
6. Rumination V0 (traverse left from Santiago's to the obvious drop and return . . .)
7. Daddy Rain 5.13 (Climb through roof past two bolts into a cave packed with Daddy Longleg Spiders which cascade over your head like a nightmare scene from Fantasia. Enjoyable.)

Less than Zero Wall (First wall past Fiji Springs.)

8. Less than Zero V0-

Andrew Lies

9. Kabob V2 (Left most problem.)

10. Nirvana V2 (Just left of tree splitting wall.)
11. The Luhan V1 (What appears obvious. Seam right of tree.)

#11 Rules
12. I Ate David V2 (Traverse right from moss, around tree and top out.)
13. #11 Rules V1 (Vertical top-out of Ate David.)
14. I Hate David V2 (Continue traverse to top out obvious seam.)

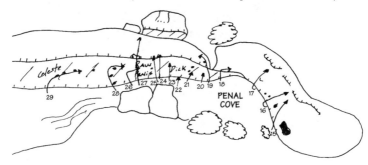

PENAL COVE

Penal Cove
15. Grapevine V2 (Feet on pedestal, move right staying low, top out on pocks.)
16. Rabbit-Eared Bandycoot V2 (Start under low roof moving up right on good ledges to pocks, meet Grapevine top out.)
17. Cane Toad V4 ♛ (Left hand mono-wrap, feet high, to 2-finger and top out direct. Ouch.)
18. Stinkfoot V3 ♛ (Sit down start. Traverse right from the low flake and top out right of the obvious hole.)
19. Stroke V4 ♛ (Begin at the one finger pocket just left of Stinkfoot, bad cling in left hand. Holds in the trough are off-route.)
20. Shwang V4+ (Start at the Dick mono and the two-finger right of Dick's holds. Crank through wall between Stroke and Dick on inad equate edges and pockets. All holds used for Dick and Stroke are off route.)
21. Dick V3 ♛ (Start with feet on the low edges. Pull the pockets right

of the graffiti, "Dick")

22. Hard Dick V4 (Start at the one finger directly under "Dick" and pull the bulge straight over)

23. Boner V7 (Pull the "Dick" bulge using only the worst holds— the lowest one finger pocket under the "K," the bad edge/mono combination left of the "D," and the bad edge left of the joined pockets at the lip. Sit down start. Any feet are on.)

24. Left of Dick V1 (Feet start hooked on boulder, pull obvious seam.)

25. Schlong V2 (Sit down, feet on skirt, pull pockets left of Left of Dick. Exit via "Left of Dick")

26. Gelding ₩ V5 (Start at Grafitti "Raw Penus" pull right under roof into large holds under Left of Dick. Holds above the lip are off route. Finish via Kevorkian (see Raw Penus).)

27. Raw Penus ₩ ₩ V6 (Start at the graffiti "Raw Penus" and climb through the roof. Finish straight up through the shallow one finger pockets. Bad landing. Another variation low traverses the "Dick" wall and pulls into the trough right of Stroke V4. Go for the Kevorkian pump by moving directly into Stinkfoot V5.)

28. Gleam in Her Eye ₩ ₩ (Start left of "Raw Penus" with a foot in the Africa-shaped pocket. Move right through buckets to join "Raw Penus" at the lip. Finish with the short low traverse to trough V4. Finish with the Kevorkian. V5. Mercy Kill V6+** starts with Raw Penis to the large pod at the end of Stinkfoot and reverses Gleam. No rest in the pod is V7. Good pump.)

29. Bone Fetish ₩ ₩ V6 (Start way left of "Gleam" at the pockets beneath the Graffiti "Celeste." Pull buckets under roof into the "Gleam Kevorkian.")

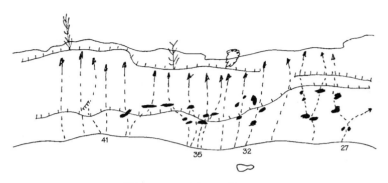

Bucket Cave Left

Bucket Cave

27. Slacker 5.13 🏵 🏵 (Grab the dog-bone and fire through the roof pausing to clip 5 bolts. Whew!)
28. Zappa V4 🏵 (Dog-bone pod start, move left through pods staying right of Rethreads holds. Bold.)
29. Rethreads V2 (Move through obvious thread-pods, right under lip, bring slings.)
30. Threads V2 (Left under lip.)

The following problems start left of the linked CH graffiti. Problems all begin with feet on the rock skirt. Variations, like bacteria, can multiply exponentially.

31. L. A. V9? (Ugly dyno to a sloping mono awaits a visit from Jerry Moffatt.)
32. Master Cylinder V6 (Through obvious hueco)
33. Icabod Crane V3 (Matching 3-finger pocks to direct exit, includes vul can for left hand.)
34. Round-up V5 (Thin pockets staying off Icabod holds.)
35. Gogol V2 (On big holds move right, top out under tree.)
36. Vom V0 (Gogol start with direct finish, better sans feet.)
37. Dead Ant V1 (Left of Vom, stay off Gogol holds.)
38. Crusoe V3 (Left and right pockets left to Big Brick, below tree.)
39. Poe V3 (Staying off big left hand, dyno up right to small brick.)

40. Rash V1 (Poe start, use big hold, direct finish.)
41. Twang V5 (Low mono through shallow two fingers to boner edge.)
42. Crackle V3 (Sit down start to layback left of Twang.)
43. Snap V3 (Big feet, small holds left of Crackle.)
44. T. O. V0 (Take pockets to direct finish.)
45. Wiener V0 (Any one of the many pocket climbs left of the boulder that leans against the down-climb ramp.)

The road of excess leads to the palace of wisdom.
Listen to the fools reproach! it is a kingly title!
Exuberance is Beauty.
Improvement makes straight roads, but the crooked roads without
Improvement, are the roads of Genius.
Where man is not nature is barren.
— William Blake, Marriage of Heaven and Hell

BULL CREEK PARK

Directions: From Town Lake, take Mopac (1) north to 2222. Exit and turn left. Follow 2222 for several miles. Turn right on Lakewood. If you pass under 360 you've gone too far. Follow Lakewood to Bull Creek Park. Park across the low water crossing. Follow the trail along the creek, downstream, until you reach the Library Wall.

General Description: The most highly concentrated, difficult limestone climbing area in Austin proper. The Library Wall offers several classic pocket climbs on an overhanging face. The proximity of the creek and configuration of the cliff, combined with a steady southern breeze make Bull Creek an ideal summer crag. Go for the triple crown (Red points of Metaphysics, Atlas Shrugged and Gulliver's in an afternoon) or attempt to walk the Library. The record for number of climbs in an afternoon is five.

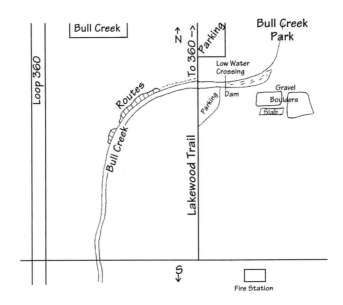

BULL CREEK OVERVIEW

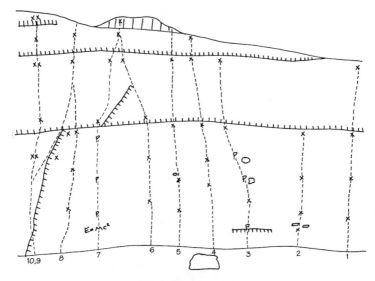

THE LIBRARY

The Library (right to left)

1. Altered States 5.12 Greg Brooks

   Project Shawn Kitzmiller (Left of Altered)

2. Gulliver's Travels 5.12+/13- ⚝ (height dependant) Jeff Jackson
3. Atlas Shrugged 5.12 ⚝ Jeff Jackson
4. Surrender 5.12 ⚝ Jack Mileski
5. Finnegan's Wake 5.13+ (project)
6. Kubla Khan 5.13 Jeff Jackson
7. Metaphysics 5.12+ ⚝ Jeff Jackson
8. Lord of the Flies 5.12 Russell Rand
9. Blatant (AKA Head Trip) 5.12- Dave Head FFA: Mike Head, Scott
   Harris, Larry Spears
10. Do the Right Thing 5.12- Jeff Jackson

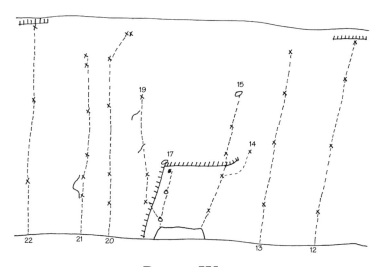

Bonzo Wall

Bonzo Wall

11. Minerva 5.11+ Elaine Catlin (Goldshuts)
12. Chemical Warfare 5.11- Greg Brooks
13. Beans and Rice 5.12- Jeff and Cristina Jackson
14. Head Thing (project) (bolts angle right.)
15. Bonzo's Revenge 5.13 Hank Caylor, Alex Catlin added finish (move
    right through the obvious pockets and straight up to the not so
    obvious finish.)

16. Project (Left of Bonzo's Revenge)
17. Bedtime for Bonzo 5.11 ⚓ (ring bolts) James Crump (Named after Hinkley's assassination attempt.)
18. Italian Route (A2) James Crump, Dave Head (Traverse right on hooks and bolts from Bonzo.)
19. Raging Bull 5.12- ⚓ Jeff Jackson (Climb the arete left of Bedtime.)
20. Boss Bull 5.12- Jeff Jackson
21. The Green Fuse 5.12- ⚓ FFA Jeff Jackson (Aid seam with bolts.)
22. Bronco 5.12 R Jeff Jackson

Rick's Traverse V hard— Traverse the lower hump from the left end to the Bonzo boulder.

Far Wall

23. Gooched 5.11 Bill Gooch (Walk to the far wall, 200 yards left of Bronco.)

"Say! Look at his fingers! One, two, three . . . How many fingers do I see? One, two, three, four, five, six, seven, eight, nine, ten. He has eleven! Eleven! This is something new. I wish I had eleven, too!"
— Doc Seuss, *One Fish Two Fish*

Bouldering

To boulder at Bull Creek, park at the dirt parking area before crossing the low water. The boulders are upstream. A nice, pea-gravel landing was recently built which cushions falls from the most popular boulder. Thanks to Parks Representative James Crump. These boulders provide great pocket climbing despite a somewhat polished veneer.

Another group of high boulders can be found farther downstream. To reach these boulders, follow the trail at the base of the bolted climbs, past a break in the wall, until another wall begins. This wall is home to Bill Gooche's 5.11, Gooched. The boulders are just downhill from this wall.

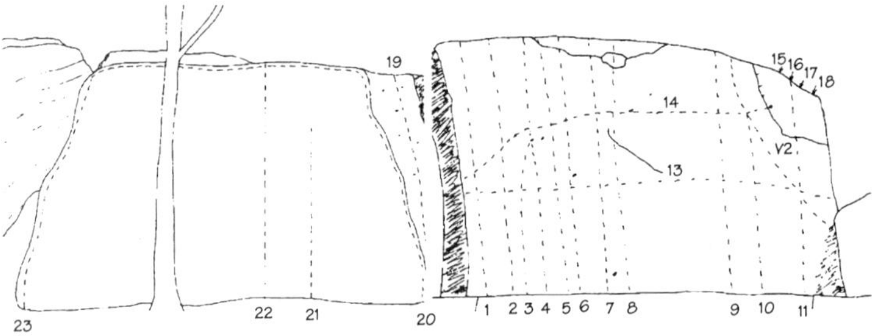

Frontside Boulders

Frontside Boulders

1. Screaming Fingers V0
2. Moss Farm V3
3. Dazzling Desperation V2
4. Short Face V2
5. Face The Face V3
6. Gitty Up V3
7. Left of Classic V1
8. Classic V0
9. Mad Dog and Beans V2
10. Bovine Perspiration V2
11. Short Man V0
12. Short Hands V3 (keep hands below the large ledge)
13. Bill Creek Traverse V4
14. Crump Traverse V4
15. Hole in the Wall V4
16. Freaking Feet V2
17. The Point V1
18. West End V0
19. Pocket Face V0
20. Layback V1
21. Walter Weed Shuffle V5 ♕
22. Tiny Dancer V7 ♕
23. Ruffles V3

> "One man's nightmare is another man's dream . . . "
>
> — John Long, *Gorilla Monsoon*

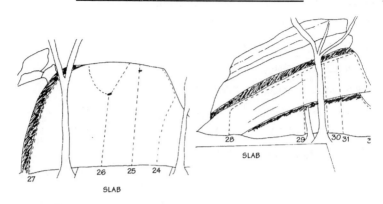

EIGEN VECTOR & BIG CHIEF BOULDERS

Eigen Vector & Big Chief Boulders

24. The Nude Edge V1 ⚘
25. Eigen Vector V6
26. Mission Impossible V4
27. Underclling V2
28. Hank Crank V2
29. A Trick of the Trade V2
30. Contrived V2
31. Squonk V2
32. Big Chief V1

MT. BONNELL

Directions: Take Mopac (1) to 2222. Exit and turn left on 2222. Left on Mt. Bonnell road. Wind uphill and park in the lot. Approach the climbs by climbing down a short trail on the north (right as you look out towards Lake Austin) end of the cliff.

General Description: Wow, Pansy, what a great view! The summer evening folds the world in its mysterious embrace. Frank and Pansy glom madly in the front seat of Dad's Volvo. Frank palms Pansy's breast. She parries with a deft right swipe honed during tennis practice last semester. They kiss again, threatening to suck each other apart. The sun sets over Lake Austin. Meanwhile, below the canyon rim . . . Limestone. Strange, orange fossile weaves.

Access: A climbing ban is sporadically enforced by police because the bourgeois, bullet-headed, million-dollar home-owners at the base of the hill are worried about falling rock. The chances of a rock falling to the base of that tree-covered hill are about the same as the head of one of those households getting a blow job from his wife. Astronomical.

(left to right)

Roof Uno

1. Last Picture Show 5.10 (4 bolts, one jammed knot) Jeff Jackson
2. Roof Uno 5.11 (TR) Right side of Roof Uno
3. Chucks 5.9 (3 bolts) Cristina Jackson

Roof Dos

4. High Times 5.11+ ♛ (5 bolts) Hank Caylor
5. Ecbatana 5.12- ♛ (Joins High Times at the anchor) Alex Catlin
6. Tree of Woe 5.12- ♛ (4 bolts) Jeff Jackson
7. Torts 5.10- ♛ (2 bolts, #2 friend for exit) Jeff Jackson

Roof Big

8. Nineveh 5.12- (Alex Catlin)
9. Aid Line (unfinished) James Crump and Dale Bergeron

"I go along with Thorkell Son of Thorkell the Misaligned and Kolbein Snub
when they sack the Irish coast and violate the Irish children, women, dogs,
and cattle and burn the Irish houses and pitch the ancient priceless Irish
manuscripts into the sea. Then I sing about it.

. . . There were thirteen of us: Thorkell Son of Thorkell the Misaligned,
Thorkell the Short, Thorkell Thorkellson, Thorkell Cat, Thorkell Flat-Nosed,
Thorkell-neb, Thorkell Ale-Lover, Thorkell the Old, Thorkell the Deep-mind-
ed, Ofeig, Skeggi, Grim and Me. We are tough. We are hardy. We are
bold."

— T. Coraghessan Boyle, "We are Norsemen"

FRANK'S MEAT MARKET

Directions: From Town Lake, follow Mopac to 2222. Exit, turn left. Stay
on 2222 to 360 west (left). Pull off 360 at the dirt parking just before the big,
arching bridge. There are several moderate top ropes on the road cut on
both sides of 360. One bolted climb exists on the south-side road cut, a 5.9, as
well as two bolted climbs downstream. These climbs were put up by Hank
Caylor.

To get to Frank's Meat Market, cross to the north side of 360 and walk up
the ramp to the top of the road cut. Cut left through the trees on a good trail
that traverses the rim of the cliff. Climb down to the base at the first obvious
down-climb. (Might be scary for wimpy sport-climbers.) Cut back toward 360
until you reach the obvious crack, roofs and faded graffiti that reads "Frank's
Meat Market."

General Description: High quality limestone. Classic, moderate crack
climbing. Frank's Meat Market is located on a hill once known as the Eagle's
Nest which was, in turn, a piece of Camp Tom Wooten, a boy scout retreat.
The Eagle's Nest overlooks a beautiful section of Lake Austin and one can only
imagine the awesome games of Capture the Flag that took place up there
before the city blasted the Eagle's Nest in half to install Loop 360. As Edward
Abbey once said, "Every boy scout troop deserves a forest to get lost, miser-
able and starving in." Well, at least there is half a hill left.

Frank's Wall

(left to right)

Left Arete 5.7

Frank's Crack 5.9 Dave Hannah (to the bolt below the roof.) Pull the roof 5.11

Frank's Meat Market 5.11 Top roped by James Crump, bolted by Jeff Jackson.

Frank's Direct 5.12 Jeff Jackson, Ian Powell, Johnny Sketch

Hacked Pocket (project?)

Gullich Problem (project)

Ian's Dihedral (project)

SEIDER CREEK

Directions: Between 34th and 38 1/2 on the east side of Shoal Creek.

General Description: One day a wild band of marauding Comanches cut down Mr. Seider and family while they slept here in their quaint, turn-of-the-century cabin. At least that's what I think the historical marker alludes to . . . More importantly, there is a great-looking traverse along the limestone hump just beside the running trail along Shoal Creek. I've been meaning to brush it down and send it for a couple of years, but I've not had a chance. The first ascent is up for grabs

GOOCH TRAVERSE — BOULDERING

Directions: Located at 29th and Lamar. Park across the street at the parking lot on the southwest corner. Cross the street and walk downstream to the cement crossing. Uphill to the boulders in the trees.

General Description: Blocky, white limestone boulders. Traverse the big boulder right to left and pull the roof for a V4 problem. Left to right staying low is V4. Several good problems and variations can be found on the overhanging, south boulder.

UNIVERSITY OF TEXAS

Waller Creek — Bouldering

Directions: Located at Martin Luther King and San Jacinto. Walk past the old oil pump and down to the creek.

General Description: Vertical limestone walls. Waller Creek was once the place to boulder. A variety of vertical problems exist at V0 to V2.

Highlights: Curved Wall Traverse V2 (South side)

Atomic Traverse V2 (Traverse the edge beneath the capstones on the south side starting at the farthest point right.)

Nuclear Traverse V3 (Traverse the edge beneath the capstones on the north side starting left.)

Straight Wall Traverse V5 (Traverse the northside wall from tree to tree.)

Arch Enemy V5 The one that got away from Crump. (Climb the right hand arch from right to left on the southside using only the keystones.)

Slubberdegullion V1 (Start Arch Enemy then move straight up.)

Aerials A1 to A3 (Various lunges have been done by using only those holds which can be reached while standing on the ground. Walk your feet up and launch for the edge beneath the capstones!)

Jester Dormitory Food Service Entrance

Amputee Crack 5.11 James Crump. Crack formed by retaining wall.

Cripple Direct 5.10 James Crump. Face by entrance.

Jester West Chimney 5.9 X Dave Head. 14 story chimney and downclimb.

PCL Library

PCL Library Chimney 5.6 X James Crump. Six stories and downclimb. Southeast corner at stairwell.

Football Stadium

Northside Dihedral 5.9 James Crump. Climb crack where Belmont joins
stadium.

Section 26 5.9 James Crump. Overhanging crack.

Northeast Sneak In Crack 5.8 James Crump.

10TH STREET BRIDGE — BOULDERING

Directions: Located at 10th street and Lamar Blvd. Park on 10th behind
the 7-11 and walk downhill under the bridge.

General Description: Limestone. Fierce, overhanging edges. Traverse
right to left V5. Finish by climbing up with the arete holds off limits. Another
Eerik Harmes (Austin Bouldering Guru) problem.

Terry's Variation V8— Stay below the line of obvious good crimpers.
Right to Left.. Lap for V9.

MOSQUITO BRIDGE — BOULDERING

Directions: From Town Lake, look for the north abutment of the railroad
tracks that cross over the Colorado. Mosquito Bridge is located near the junc-
tion of Lamar and First Street.

General Description: Two cracks. One 5.8 hand crack and one 5.10- finger crack. Barry Wilson is responsible for the name because these cracks are
small and vicious and make you bleed. Another Eerik Harmes discovery.

SUNKEN GARDENS — BOULDERING

Directions: From Town Lake, head south on Lamar, turn west onto
Barton Springs. Turn left at Robert E. Lee and park at one of the baseball dia-
monds. Walk downhill to the spring-fed pool.

General Description: Long traverse walls. Old-school climbing hang.
Limestone blocks. Edges. Long traverses that will build forearm strength as
well as footwork.

Variations:

Low Traverse on Upper Left Wall V4 (Stay below all handholds used for
the regular traverse.)

Center Wall Above the Seam V4 (All holds on and below the high seam
that runs the length of the Center Wall are off limits.)

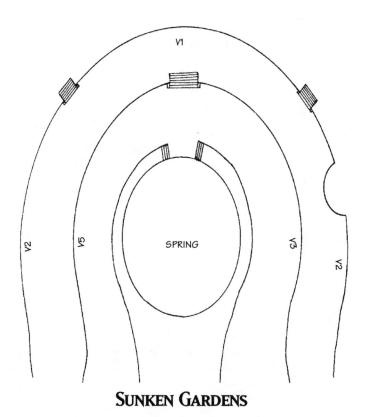

SUNKEN GARDENS

Non-Commercial Barton Springs Underwater Bouldering

Directions: Find the Barton Springs Pool run-off. (Look for a motley
assortment of miserable-looking people; Bums, dogs and scabby children.)
Wade in and find the obvious crack system that extends from the left side of
the spillway into the creek. Start at the bottom of the system and climb
upstream to the spillway. One breath. V5

Thanks Bluebeard for showing us this one.

Gena Scurry, Texas Limestone   Photo by Benji Fink

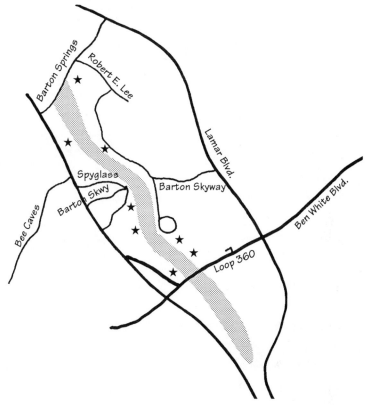

BARTON CREEK OVERVIEW

BARTON SPRINGS AREA

Directions: From Town Lake, head south on Lamar and turn right at Barton Springs. Turn left into the Barton Springs Pool parking lot. Park at the south end close to the Hillside theater. Follow the trail out of the south end of the lot.

General Description: Great stone.

Ka'nee Knee's Wall
(The first boulder-sized limestone sanctuary. Marked by a tree that grows on the right and arches over the trail. Ultra-classic bouldering)

1. Ka'nee Knee's Bane ☠☠ V3 (Start in the horizontal crack and pull the right-hand roof. Traverse left)
2. O Risk a Knee ☠ V3 (Start at Ka'nee Knee's Bane and low-traverse left. Tree is off-route. Use tricks.)
3. Orbit V3 (Pull left end of Ka'nee Knee's Roof and reverse Ka'nee Knee's Bane.)
4. Tunnel Vision V3 (Start in the cave left of the tree.)

Rappeler's Wall
(Clean gray waterstreak that splits the foliage a quarter mile past Ka'nee Knee's. Climbs from 5.6 to 5.9+.)
The Sink ☠ V2 (Short cave at ground level, just left of the Rapeler's Wall.)
The Plumber V3 (Exit the Sink right on thin side clings.)

Wasp Wall (Next forty foot wall. Somewhat overgrown.)
(right to left)
5. Classic 5.4 (Dihedral)
6. Holtzendorf Direct 5.7 Harold Holtzendorf (Named for Harold Holtzendorf, an Austin climber that died soloing Lubrication in Estes Park, Colorado. He is sorely missed.)
7. Mosquito 5.9+ James Crump
8. Wasp 5.8 Crump
9. Rush 5.10 Crump
10. Atomic Rush 5.10+ Bill and Paul Horton

Balrog Wall
(Next big wall with house on top.)
11. Zipper Lounge 5.10- (Obvious dihedral. Named after Austin's first all-nude titty bar. Now the location of the head shop, Planet K, on South Lamar.) Garth McGee
12. Rocket Pocket 5.10+ ☠ Crump

13. Balrog 5.11- Crump
14. Head Trip 5.11 Dave Head
15. Tit Scratch 5.11 Crump
16. The McClure/Sanders V3 (Traverse the sloping lower band)

Zilker Soccer Field Problem V2+ 👑 👑 (Bold. Located across Barton Springs road on the rock island in the middle of the soccer fields. This problem ascends the steep northeast wall over the spot where the Shakespeare in the Park performances take place. First Ascent: Bill Gooch.)

CAMPBELL'S HOLE

Directions: From Town Lake, Drive south on Mopac and Exit Barton Skyway. Turn Left. Follow Barton Skyway until it deadends. Stop n' Go on the left. Park and follow the trail behind the guard rail. At the T, turn left. The west bank rises on the far side of Barton Creek.

General Description: Often dry swiming hole. Mucho U. T. tanning beauties.

West Bank
(left to right)
17. Holy Diver 5.12 👑   Hank Caylor
18. Gravity's Angel 5.11 Calvin Hiser

NEW WALL

Directions: Same as Campbell's Hole. At the T in the trail turn right. Follow a good trail aproximately half a mile. The cliff is on the east side of Barton Creek. Climbs labeled from left to right.

General Description: Steep. Gunky. Blocky. Limestone of the pumpy variety. Excellent training wall.

Bouldering: Left of Flintstones find an abundance of good traversing in a cave. The limestone hump uphill and left of the Traverse Cave also has a nice traverse that goes at V2.

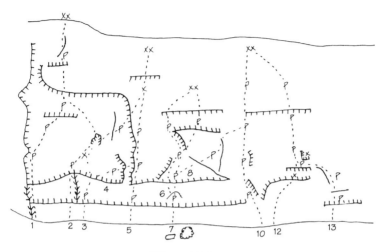

NEW WALL

New Wall

1. Meet the Flintstones 5.9 Dave Cardosa, Greg Brooks, Scott Harris
2. Mr. Slate 5.11- Brooks, Cardosa, Harris
3. Yabba Dabba Do 5.11- Harris, Cardosa, Brooks
4. Schoolboy Indirect 5.9
5. Schoolboy Fantasies 5.10+ Greg Brooks, Robert Middleton (Climb the layback crack.)
6. Cloud Nine 5.11 Adam Hurst
7. Hysteria 5.11- ☙Adam Hurst, Scott Harris, Dave Cardosa, Hank Caylor
8. Lots of People 5.11 Rick Watson, Tony Faucett
9. Eraser Head 5.12- Harris, Cardosa, Caylor
10. Mandingo 5.11+ Harris, Cardosa, Caylor
11. Mandingo Direct 5.11+
12. Buddha 5.12- ☙ Jeff Jackson, bolted by Greg Brooks
13. Walk the Dog 5.11 ☙ Caylor, Cardosa, Harris
14. Rabbit Hut 5.11 Rick Watson (Starts on Walk the Dog and traverses left at the third bolt. Finish at the chains on Flintstones. Long slings.)
15. Wowie Zowie 5.11- Hank Caylor
Access 5.6

Terrace

(The Terrace refers to the climbs between the New and Great Wall.)

16. Crystal New Persuasion 5.10 ♛ Calvin Hiser

17. Cactus Patch 5.10- Tony Faucett

Access 5.7

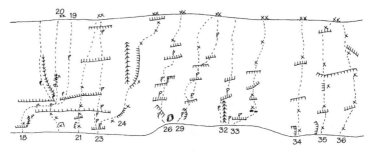

GREAT WALL

Great Wall

18. Heaven Can Wait 5.11- Scott Harris, Dave Cardosa

19. Heaven's Gate 5.11 Harris, Cardosa

20. Hug Thy Mother 5.12 Tony Faucett

21. Disneyland 5.13 Alex Catlin

22. Wind Chimes A2 Cardosa, Brooks

23. Iron Man 5.12 Harris, Cardosa, Greg Brooks

24. Magical Mystery Tour/Pee Wee's Big Adventure 5.11+ Harris, Cardosa

25. Adams Way 5.12 T.R. (Named for Adam Hurst, an Austin climber killed by lightning on the Naked Edge in Eldorado, Colorado. He is still sorely missed.) Adam Hurst

26. Through the Looking Glass 5.11- ♛ Cardosa, Harris, Brooks

27. Tunnel Vision Direct 5.12- ♛ Jeff Jackson

28. Girlie Vision 5.11 Jack Lawrence (Avoid the Tunnel Vision crux by moving left to the large side cling.)

29. Tunnel Vision 5.11+ ♛ Dave Cardosa, Scott Harris (Move right instead of pulling the left hand bulge at the bolt.)

30. Eye of the Storm 5.11- Brooks, Cardosa (Move right at second clip of

Tunnel Vision and finish Power Monkey.)
31. Shock the Monkey 5.12 Dave Cardosa (Move left after the second clip of Power Monkey and finish Tunnel Vision Direct.)
32. Power Monkey 5.12+ Dave Cardosa, Scott Harris
33. Space Cowboy 5.12- ♛ Caylor, Cardosa, Harris

Geritol Wall
34. Sunshine Boys 5.11 Scott Harris
35. Rock and Roll High School 5.11- Scott Harris
36. Cedar Fever 5.10+ ♛ Scott Harris

Random Walls
The Random Walls refer to those walls just downstream from the Great Wall.
37. Gunsmoke 5.10 ♛ Cristina Jackson (Classic grey prow, fifty yards downstream from Space Cowboy.)
38. Hank's 5.10 Hank Caylor (White face with bolts, one hundred yards from Gunsmoke.)
39. Tiddlywinks 5.9 X Jeff Jackson (Twenty five foot stacked formation in the trees close to Hank's.)

GUS FRUH

Directions: From Town Lake, head south on Lamar Blvd. and turn right on Barton Skyway. Left on Barton Hills at stop sign. Park at the wooden sign on the right that reads "Gus Fruh". Follow a clear trail downhill. Cross Barton creek and turn right. The cliff rises just off the trail.

General Description: Classic gray stone with big features. A good place to learn limestone technique. Only traditional tactics are tolerated here. Lines go up on lead with a minimal amount of bolting. If you employ new-wave tactics, ie. rap bolting, chipping, etc ... your bolts will be chopped. 'Nuff said. Some climbs require nuts (in both senses of the word.)

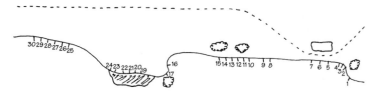

GUS FRUH TOPO

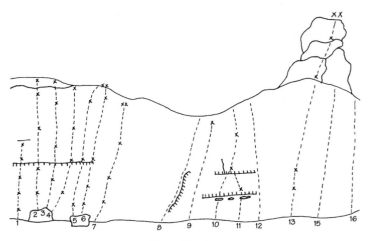

GUS FRUH

Gus Fruh

(left to right)

1. Running Man 5.12- Scott Harris, Dave Cardosa
2. Reefer Madness 5.11 ♛ Scott Harris
3. Cyborg 5.11 ♛ Scott Harris
4. Birdland 5.10+ Jeff Jackson (Retro-bolted.)
5. Iranian Arms Deal 5.8 Keith Guillory, David Renberg
6. Fern Bar 5.9 Keith Guillory
7. Gros Ventre (Big Stomach) 5.10 Dave Cardosa
8. Wyoming Women 5.8 ♛ (crack) George Hazzard

variation: Heir Apparant 5.9 (top rope two feet right of Wyoming
    Women.)

variation: Wandering Women 5.9 (Climb the first half of Wyoming

Women and traverse up and right and finish Thumb Dance.)

9. Chicken Supreme 5.10 (Climbs to gully left of two bulges.)

variation: Betwixt 5.11 Ralph Showalter (Climb straight over bulge just right of Chicken.)

variation: Egg Salad Sandwich 5.10 (Climb right side of bulge between Trash-can Man.)

10. Trash-can Man 5.11- Hank Caylor

11. Rock Retard 5.11- ♛ Scott Harris, Randy Spears, Mike Head

12. Apostrophe 5.11 Rick Watson (Avoid big holds to the left.)

13. Thumb Dance 5.10 ♛♛ John Sanders (The classic Gus Fruh must-do.)

14. Blind Date 5.11 Dave Cardosa

15. Praying Mantle 5.10 Ralph Showalter

16. Rent a Pig 5.10 Ralph Showalter (Climb marked by hangerless bolt right of Praying.)

17. 5.5

18. Access 5.4

Traverse— Start at Reefer Madness and traverse V5. Low traverse V6.

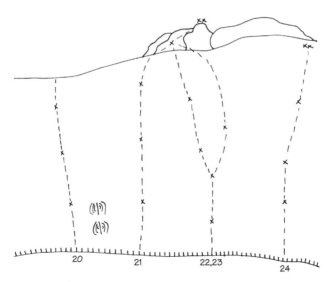

KINGDOM OF GING

Kingdom of Ging

19. Hank's B8— V7 ♛
20. Charlie Don't Surf 5.10+ Scott Harris, Dave Cardosa
21. Jerry's Kids 5.11 ♛ Hank Caylor, Scott Harris
22. Sex Dwarfs 5.11 Steve Languell (First Top Rope Ascent, Dave Cardosa)
23. King of Ging 5.10- ♛ Hank Caylor
24. Gray Streak 5.10- Tony Faucett, René Payne

Guide's Wall

(left to right)

The Guide's Wall is located roughly seventy-five feet to the right of the Kingdom of Ging.

25. Bulge 5.9 Goomba John Sanders, Lauren Clayton (Climb the over hanging bulge on the left end of the wall.)
26. Thin Crack 5.5 John Sanders, Lauren Clayton
27. Flash Crack 5.6 John Sanders, Lauren Clayton

variation: Stand-off 5.9 Ralph Showalter (Climb thin seam left of April Fool staying off Flash Crack.)

28. April Fool 5.9+ ♛ Ralph Showalter (Exit to the left of the cave.)
29. Touch of Class 5.7 ♛ John Sanders, Lauren Clayton (Wide Crack.)
30. Steep Bulge 5.10 (Bulge right of Touch of Class.)

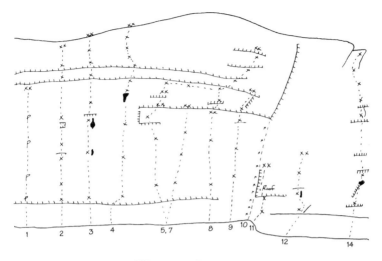

URBAN ASSAULT

URBAN ASSAULT

Directions: From the Gus Fruh Access cross Barton Creek and turn left on the well marked trail. Urban Assault is the big white buttress on the west side of the creek. If Barton Creek is high, it is possible to bushwack up the west bank.

General Description: Steep face. Big roofs. Premium on all around technique, from dime edges to big slopes.

Left Oven

1. Ladrone (Thief) 5.11 Paul Clark
2. Masada 5.12 Paul Clark
3. Femme 5.13 Kevin Gallagher
4. Starfish 5.12 ♛ Jeff Jackson
5. Cell Block 5.11 ♛ Russell Rand
6. Medicine Man 5.12 Jeff Jackson (Climb Cell Block and move right. Finish Techtonics.)
7. Mah Jong 5.12 Karen Rand
8. Plate Techtonics 5.13 ♛ Jeff Jackson
9. Spelioantics (project)

10. Urban Assault 5.10+ or A1 James Crump

Right Oven

11. Deep Flow 5.13- Jeff Jackson
12. Mandibles 5.12 ❦ Rick Watson
13. Lydesaid A1 Tom Lyde
14. Manchild 5.12 Jeff Jackson (Climb closed when the owl is home.)
Excellent boulder problems at creek level to the right.

"The brain has the power to control all,
think positive you'll be unable to fall . . ."

— Ice T., "Mind Over Matter"

Airman's Cave

Directions: Airman's Cave is located almost directly across from the 5.8 Sanctuary. Squeeze into this tight cave and go.

General Description: Hey man, let's go do Airman's Cave! Airman's cave is a recommended stop for the hardcore adventurer. Like a good off-width crack, this squeeze cave (there's only three places where you can stand up) tests mental limits. A roundtrip excursion, which winds under Whole Foods, Loop 360, and Southwood Mall, should take something in the neighborhood of twenty hours. Not for claustrophobes. Entering the cave under the influence of blotter acid has changed the ways of many a sinner.

A descent through Airman's Cave has been compared to the difficulty encountered on a 5.11+ climb. Bill Russell and Tom Bird are rumored to have made the first complete roundtrip journey.

5.8 SANCTUARY / SEISMIC WALL

Directions: Take Mopac (1) south to 360. Exit 360 west. Take 360 west under Mopac and continue to a stoplight. Turn left and park at the Barton

Creek access trail. Walk down the trail until you can see the wall across the creek. This is the Seismic Wall, named for the ground shaking boulders that fell during the first attempts at cleaning. The 5.8 Sanctuary is located about a quarter of a mile downstream, on the same side as the Seismic Wall.

General Description: The Seismic Wall is worth a visit if only to check out the funky orange rock. Recently, someone bolted the hell out of this place. Who? We don't know. The Sanctuary is a good place for the beginner to practice gear placement.

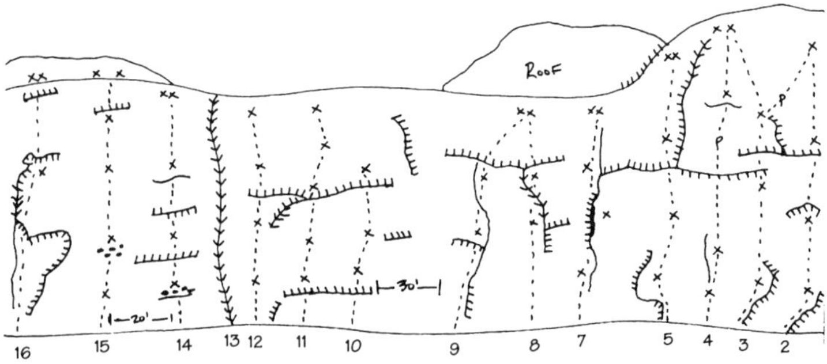

SEISMIC WALL

Seismic Wall

(Right to Left)

1. Hollywood 5.5 ♛ TR Ralph Showalter (Low angle open book.)
2. 5.7 Bolts
3. 5.8 Bolts
4. 5.8 Bolts
5. 5.9 (Corner) Bolts
6. 5.9 TR ♛ (off left anchors)
7. 5.10- Bolted layback
8. 5.10 Bolts (Lonesome Dove 5.12 TR out roof)
9. 5.10+ Bolts
10. 5.11 Bolts missing first hanger
11. 5.11 ♛ Bolts
12. 5.11 Bolts missing all hangers
13. Seismic Step 5.6 ♛ Dihedral (Keith Guillory)

14. 5.10 Bolts

15. 5.10- Bolts w/ wide anchors

16. 5.9 bolts

5.8 Sanctuary

(quarter mile past (downstream) Seismic Wall, left to right)

6. Fist Crack 5.7

7. Face Off 5.9 (finger crack)

8. Lots of Bouldering

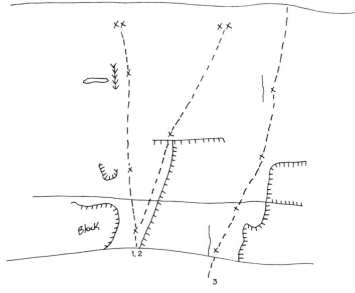

KIRK AND ALVIN'S WALL

Kirk and Alvin's Wall

(left to right)

Directions: See Seismic Wall. Approach this wall by parking at the 360
 access to the Greenbelt. Walk north (downstream) down Barton
 Creek. Pass Airman's cave and look for this wall on the righthand
 (east) bank.

1. Bloody Butt 5.9 (Kirk Holladay, Alvin Pons. 3 bolts, anchors, 35'.)

2. Skank Hole 5.9+ ♛ (Kirk Holladay, Alvin Pons. Start sitting in the low

cave. Angle left. 2 or 3 bolts, anchors, 40'.)
3. Pay Dirt 5.10+ ☙ (Kirk Holladay, Alvin Pons. Start sitting in cave. Straight up. 4 bolts, anchors, 45'.)
4. X-rated Negro 5.10 (Top rope the overhanging face 20' right of Pay Dirt.)

Beehive Wall
(Left to right)
Directions: See Seismic Wall. Park at the 360 access to the Greenbelt and walk south (upstream) up Barton Creek. Cross under 360 and continue upstream about 1/2 mile to this wall distinguished by a large beehive.
1. Dirty Rotten Whore 5.12- (Alvin Pons, Kirk Holladay. 5 bolts, anchors.)
2. Cardosa Route 5.12? (Dave Cardosa. Bolts.)

"In climbing where the danger is great, all attention has to be given the ground step by step, leaving nothing for beauty by the way. But this care, so keenly and narrowly concentrated, is not without advantages. One is thoroughly aroused. Compared with the alertness of the senses and corresponding precision and power of the muscles on such occasions, one may be said to sleep the rest of the year. The mind and body remain awake for some time after the dangerous ground is passed, so that arriving on the summit with the grand outlook— all the world spread below— one is able to see it better, and brings to the feast a far keener vision, and reaps richer harvest than would have been possible ere the presence of danger summoned him to life."

— John Muir

REIMER'S FISHING RANCH

Directions: From Town Lake follow Mopac south to Southwest Parkway. Turn right. When Southwest Parkway deadends into 71, turn right. Turn left onto Ranch Road 3238 (Hamilton's Pool Road) and continue for 13-14 miles. Turn right at a white sign that reads "Milton Reimer's Fishing Ranch." Follow the dirt road, staying left, to a gate. Open and close gate and pay two dollars per person at the house. Continue on, staying left and park at the Sano-can.

General Description: Limestone pockets. Beautiful setting. Especially suited to climbs in the 5.10 to 5.11 range. Excellent stone.

Camping: Camping is no longer allowed at Reimers. Camp at Pace Bend.

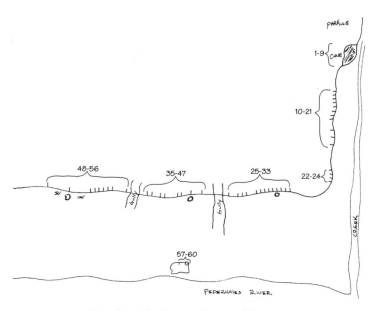

REIMER'S LEFT BAND TOPO

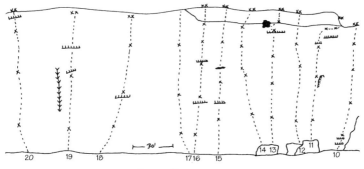

SEX CANYON

Sex Cave and Canyon

(right to left)

1. Spider Grind 5.11 Dave Cardosa, Tom and Chris Suler (First climb on the right before the Sex Cave. Traverses left.)

Variation: Mud Lip 5.11 (Spider Grind Direct, Russell Rand)

2. Sex Grind project. (Traverse left from Spider Grind to the seventh bolt on Liposuction.)

3. Viper 5.12 tr (Climb the verticle seep right of Body Wax. Exit to the Spider Grind anchors.)

4. Body Wax 5.12 ₩ Jeff Jackson (4 bolts. Climb nobby stalactites through roof)

5. Lucky Strikes 5.13 ₩ Mike Klein

6. Head 5.12+ ₩ Greg Brooks (4 bolts. Climbs the pocket face left of Body Wax.)

7. Liposuction 5.12- ₩ ₩ Greg Brooks (Traverse the lip of the obvious roof to huge stalactite. Finish up and right.)

8. Lipo Variation 5.12 Russell and Karen Rand (Continue left from dish rest finishing out E Man.)

9. Elephant Man 5.13 (broken holds) Duane Raleigh (Traverse the stalactites under the big roof.)

10. Mistaken Identity 5.11+ ₩ Greg Brooks (Black streak right of Telegraph.)

11. Telegraph Road 5.11 ₩ Greg Brooks (Approximately twenty

yards past the Sex Cave the wall grows again to thirty feet.
Telegraph starts off large boulders. Follow flake system and traverse
right under roof to finish.)

12. Sangre de Muertos 5.11 Joe Shulak
13. Let Them Eat Flake 5.12- ♛ Jeff Jackson
14. Love is a Fist 5.12 Josh Pierce
15. Learning to Fly 5.12 Jimmy Menendez
16. Learning to Crawl 5.12 Greg Brooks (Climb through the nest of
    stalactites to a blocky finish.)
17. No Recess 5.12 Wayne Crill
18. Coletrane (project)
19. Alvin's 5.12 Alvin Pons
20. Repulsive Attila 5.12 Alex Catlin
21. Snuff the Rooster 5.11- Steve Hunt, Mack Hargrave

Zoe's Wall

Located around the corner from Learning to Crawl on a shelf. Access via
a low trail. Toprope anchors and bolts.

22. I Never Called You a Beast 5.6 Greg Brooks
23. Maggie's Farm 5.6 Greg Brooks
24. Zoe's First Step 5.7 ♛ Greg Brooks

"The sun did not shine. It was too wet to play. So we sat in the house all
that cold, cold, wet day. I sat there with Sally. We sat there, we two.
And I said, "How I wish we had something to do!" Too wet to go out and
too cold to play ball. So we sat in the house. We did nothing at all. So
all we could do was to Sit! Sit! Sit! Sit! And we did not like it. Not
one little bit."

— Doctor Seuss, *Cat in the Hat*

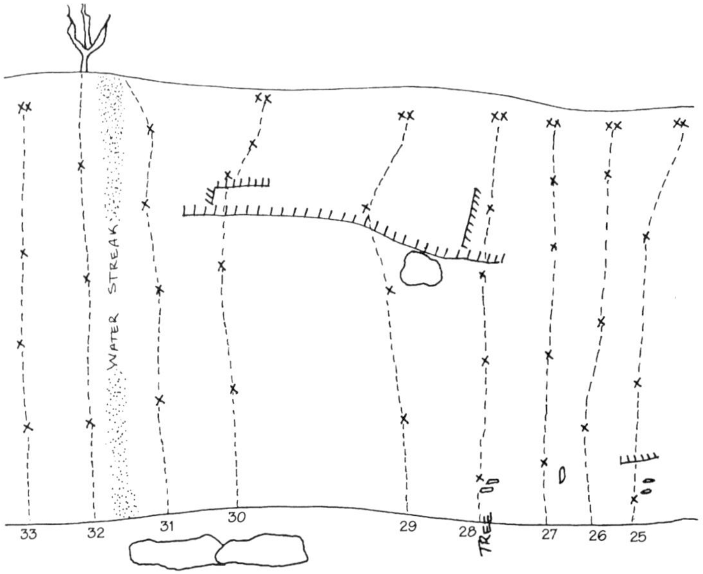

Dead Cats

Dead Cats

(Right to Left. Follow trail through the canyon and turn right along cliff. The following climbs are marked by obvious boulders on the trail and a tree growing out of the base of the wall.)

24a. Bolted Like Mex 5.10 Kevin Bentz, Stephanie Bryant (R. of Centipede.)

24b. Hilti Hiway 5.10 Bentz, Bryant

24c. Sidewinder 5.10+ Bentz (Arete)

25. Centipede 5.11- Dave Cardosa, Duane Cardosa, Tom Suler (First bulging pocket climb. Top rope anchors are located up and right of climb.)

26. Power Snatch 5.10+ (Jay Stein)

27. Reimerama 5.10- Scott and Jean Hudson (Start right of the tree.)

28. Almost Nothing to It 5.9 Sharon O'Keefe, John Parsons (Start off the tree growing out of the wall.)

29 My Name is Mud 5.9 (Curtis Mai)

30. Dead Cats 5.10 ♛ Dave Cardosa (Choice orange streak with slope

finish.)

31. 5.9

32. Water Ballet 5.10 ♛ Scott and Jean Hudson (Waterstreak left of Dead Cats.)

33. 5.9

34. Digitron 5.10+ (This climb is located on the tall boulder downhill from Dead Cats. Look for the bolted slab.)

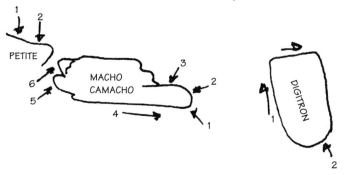

THE CAMANCHOS

The Camachos

These two boulders are located downhill of Dead Cats, right of Digitron.

The Macho Camacho

1. Rico Camacho V2 (Sit down and slap the arete, up the seam.)
2. Buck Camacho V3 (Sit down a little right of Rico and pull the bulge straight up.)
3. Rex Camacho V2(Sit down right of Buck and pull edges left and up.)
4. Traverse the Pedernales Slab High and Low V0
5. Mano Camacho V0 (Hand crack on the far corner.)
6. Dedo Camacho V2 (Sit down with right hand and foot on an arete. Pull left into finger crack.)

The Petite Camacho
(Just right of Macho.)

1. Suave Camacho V1 (Start right under vines and move left via small

edges to lip buckets.)

2. Cool Beans Camacho V7 (Start with hands on the lowest holds in the center of The Petite. Get your feet on. Jump.)

Digitron Bouldering

1. Traverse Any of the Large Sides V1
2. Digitalia V6 (Climb the steep Pedernales side of the Digitron Boulder. Very bad landing. Find threads at the top for T.R. protection.)

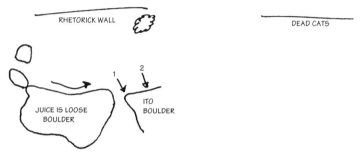

RHETORICK BOULDERING

Rhetorick Wall

This is the next series of bolted routes 40ft. left of Dead Cats Wall.

35. Punctuation Mark 5.12- (Rick Watson)
36. Rhetorick 5.12- (Rick Watson)
37. Bad Language 5.12- R (Climb through two bolts and exit left, ignoring anchors. Poor bolting job.)
38. Rags to Riches 5.11- Scott and Jean Hudson (Left of Rhetorick Wall. Rusty pins.)

The Juice is Loose V3 ₩₩ (Traverse the obvious limestone lump behind and below the Rhetorick Wall.)

The Ito Boulder (Left of Juice is Loose)

1. Lance It V0 (Sit down and pull the arete. Bad landing.)
2. Me Ito V0 (Sit down left of the arete.)

Climbs 39 - 60 are located left of the obvious gulley.

39. Cliptomania 5.11- Scott and Jean Hudson

40. Ferntasm 5.10

41. Fearless 5.10- (Follows the line in the center and right of an obvious dihedral.)

42. Grip Clip 5.12- Jeff Fanaros (Left face of dihedral.)

43. Flea Circus 5.11 ♕ Rick Watson

44. T-roofic Detour 5.10+ ♕ Jean and Scott Hudson (Move right under a big roof to orange rock above.)

45. Incredible Journey 5.12- ♕ Greg Brooks (Traverse the overlap left of T-roofic and pull the high, gray bulge. Watch for poison ivy.)

46. Rust Never Seeps 5.12 ♕ Jeff Jackson, Greg Brooks (Physical rust waterstreak.)

47. Nobody's Hero 5.10+ Benji Fink (Tall gray face just right of Tit For Tom roofs.)

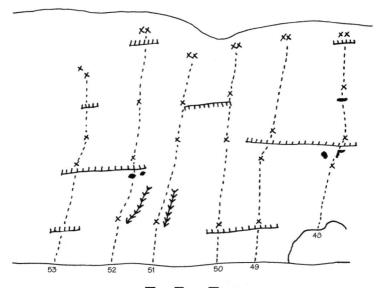

TIT FOR TOM

Tit For Tom Wall
(Excellent, steep wall 1/4 mile left of Rust.)

48. Underdog 5.10+ ✿ Benji Fink

49. Beelzebubba 5.11 ✿ J. D. Fant

50. Nuerotica 5.12- ✿ Joe Shulak

51. Mikey Likes It 5.10- ✿✿ Joe Shulak

52. Tit for Tom 5.11 Dave Cardosa, Tom Suler

53. Mother Buddha 5.11 ✿ Clayton Reagan

The Hand Beyond Wall
(Well left of Mother Buddha)

53a. Deception Pass 5.10 Kevin Bentz, Stephanie Bryant

53b. Overlord 5.12 KB, SB (Shares anchor w/ Deception)

53c. Ten Foot Pole 5.11+ Kim Duran, David Black, KB

54. Bluebeard 5.10 Barry Wilson, Kevin Gallagher

54a. Hidden Agenda 5.11 KB, SB (R. of Bluebeard)

54b. Antonioan 5.9+

54c. Go For the Jugular 5.10 KB, SB

54d Monkey Boy 5.11 KB, SB

54e. Ezra's Shelf 5.10 SB, KB

55. Daddy's Girl 5.10 Mack Hargrave

55a. Booger Boy 5.10 KB, SB

56. Harelipped Dog 5.10 Mack Hargrave

56a. San Antonio Drillers 5.10+

56b. 5.9+ San Antonio Route

56c. 5.10+ Steve Hunt, Kevin Bentz

56d. 5.10 Another S. A. Route

56e. Shadowman 5.11- KB, SB (Rappel tree to descend)

56f. Yet Another S. A. Route 5.10

World's Greatest Boulder
Many boulder problems and variations have been done to the left of Screaming Yellow Zonkers.

57. Screaming Yellow Zonkers V1 (Climb the pocketed face left of

Pocket Rocket. TR anchors on top.)

58. Pocket Rocket 5.10+ ♛ Scott and Jean Hudson (2 bolts. Follow horizontals on the left side of this boulder.)
59. Size Ain't Shit 5.11+ ♛ Charlie Chapman (Between Pocket & Shack)
60. Love Shack 5.12 ♛ Paul Clark, Jeff Jackson (2 bolts. One finger crank to edges. This line has been 4th classed.)

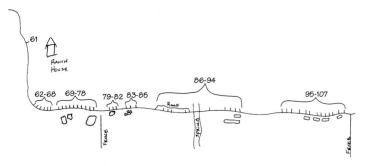

REIMER'S RIGHT BAND TOPO

Downstream Bouldering

To find this incredible band of primo bouldering drive past the Sano-can and continue down to the river. Park at one of the pullouts. Walk downstream. There are many problems already completed and many, many more to be done. See you there.

Right Band

61. Pika Peak 5.10 (Across the canyon from Let Them Eat Flake. 3 bolts. Kevin Bentz, David Black)
61a. Dos Vatos 5.10+ Kevin Bentz (R. of Pika)

Teva Slab 5.5-5.9 The Teva Slab is a low angle boulder located at the mouth of the canyon that seperates the left and right bands. Good friction practice. Harder in Teva Sandals.

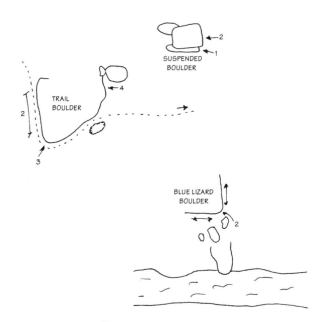

BOULDERING

Trail Boulder

This is the boulder you squeeze past on the way to Prototype.

1. Traverse Both Sides V2
2. The Creek Side V0 - V2
3. Trail Bend Corner Left V1, Right V2 (Powerful top-outs.)
4. Backside V0 (Pull obvious roof.)

Suspended Boulder

Find this boulder uphill and towards Prototype.

1. Suspended Boulder Left V2 (Start on the lower left leg of the boulder in the cave. Traverse hand crack, pull the lip and climb the face.
2. Suspension of Disbelief V2 (Start on right lip. Pull edges to summit.)

Doctor Seus Wall

This is the first concentration of bolted routes left of the Prototype Wall. (Left to right.)

62. Smitten Psychopath 5.9 (Obvious arete100 yards left of Prototype.

Curtis Mai)

63. Buttered Side Up 5.10+ (Roof. Josh Pierce)

64. Project

65. Toilet Solo 5.9 (Dirty access. Josh Pierce)

66. Socks on Chicks 5.10- (Todd McCray)

67. Blowing Smoke at the Monkey 5.11- (Curtis Mai)

68. Buttered Side Down 5.11 (Josh Pierce. Just left of Wrecking Ball.)

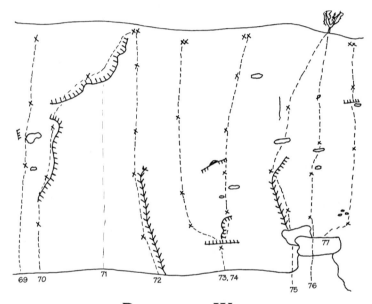

PROTOTYPE WALL

Prototype Wall

69. Wreckin' Ball 5.11 Jungleman

70. 8 Flake 5.8 ♜ ♜

71. Bisector 5.9 Curtis Mai

72. Clone Call 5.10- Scott and Jean Hudson (Dihedral with bolts.)

73. Mas Cerveza 5.11 ♜ ♜ Rick Watson (Start on a bulge. Marked by chains at the finish.)

74. Prototype 5.10+ ♜ Jean and Scott Hudson (Left of Bolt Talk.)

75. Bolt Talk 5.11- ♜ Jean and Scott Hudson (Follow seam up the

center of the face to knobs at the finish.)

76. Unnatural Selection 5.11- Jean and Scott Hudson (Start on boulder right of Bolt Talk.)

77. Bongo Fury 5.11 ☼ Rick Watson (Start on boulder and traverse right into pockets. Straight up to red shuts.)

78. Bongo Direct 5.13 (Start off the ground. Boulder is off-route.)

Blue Lizzard Boulder

Largest boulder below Prototype near the banks of the Pedernales.

1. Traverse Left to Right and Reverse V1

2. The Blue Lizzard V2+ (Sit down on corner, pull mono and shallow pockets to summit.)

3. On the Pedernales Side Find Several Problems V0 - V2 and Several V0's on the Right Side.

Mai Tai Wall

79. Tree 5.9 ☼ (unknown)

80. Mega Lounge 5.8 (Curtis Mai, Joe Shulak)

81. Let the Wallies Loose 5.9 (Curtis Mai, Joe Shulak)

82. I Speak For the Trees 5.10- (Curtis Mai, Joe Shulak)

Fern Wall

83. Pocket Change 5.10+ Scott Hudson

84. Crack Attack 5.10+ ☼ Jean and Scott Hudson (Start in a corner system and climb the right arching crack, pulling the face above.)

85. Power Pig 5.12- Cristina Jackson (Lean across a gap and climb through ferns to a nice face above.)

86. Wild Spider 5.13 ☼ (Mike Kline)

87. Reptile (Black tufa project.)

88. Dragonfly 5.12+ ☼ (Wayne Crill)

89. Ship of Fools 5.12- ☼ Russell Rand (Walk past fern-covered overhangs. Ship of Fools climbs the ramp where the overhangs end, left

of the big roofs.)

90. Ivy League 5.11 Russell Rand (Cross a spring and look uphill. Ivy League climbs the face to the right of the spring. Poison ivy.)

House of Pain

Climbs 91 - 94 are marked by a large boulder shelf to the right of the trail.

91. House of Pain 5.13 ♛ Jeff Jackson (Start at the two-finger pocket and pull the roof and overhanging face above.)

92. Rain Dance 5.12 ♛ Russell Rand (Climb the center of the House of Pain buttress.)

93. Stranglehold 5.12 ♛ Greg Brooks (Bolts right of Rain Dance.)

94. Velcro Rodeo 5.12- R Jeff Jackson (Heave to hueco and run.)

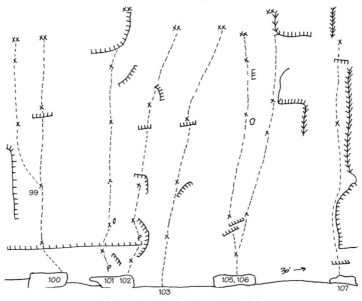

CRANKENSTEIN WALL

Crankenstein Wall

95. Ant Encounters 5.11- Tom and Chris Suler

96. Teenage Parties 5.11- Rick Watson, Tony Faucett (Left of War on Rugs. Difficult roof start.)

97. War on Rugs 5.10 ♛ Scott and Jean Hudson (Starts off the large

flake and climbs the pocketed face above.)

98. You Bet Arete 5.12- (Kevin Gallagher?)

99. Gang Bang Variation 5.11

100. Gang Bang 5.11- Jeff Jackson (Start atop boulder. Leap from right hand flake to flakes above.)

101. Crankenstein 5.11+ 🖋🖋 Scott Hudson (Marked by a low piton and initial mossy rock. Boulders at the base.)

102. Industrial Disease 5.12 Greg Brooks (Bolts right of Crankenstein.)

103. The Munchies 5.11+ Paul Irby, Wayne Crill

104. Squirrell Cage TR anchors

105. Short Term Memory Loss 5.11 Rick Watson

106. Wife in the Fast Lane 5.10+ Jean Hudson (Stem off a boulder to start white face. Move left under roof to chains.)

107. Back Off Crack 5.9 🖋 Injinio Jones (One bolt protects face move.)

More bouldering downstream from the left band.

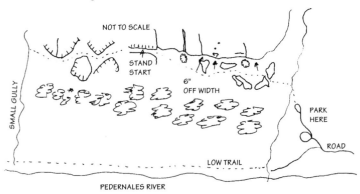

BOULDERING SECTION I

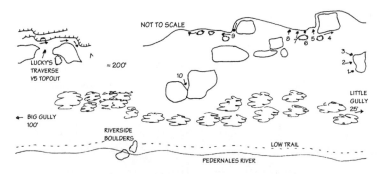

BOULDERING SECTION II

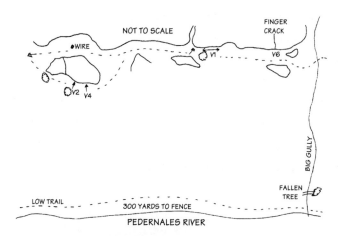

BOULDERING SECTION III

PACE BEND PARK

Directions: Mopac south to Southwest Parkway. Turn Right. At highway 71, turn right. At FM 2322 turn right and follow the road to Pace Bend Park.

General Description: Ah summer! 100 degrees. The air conditioners spit and whine. Westlake housewives stand fossilized in their cool museums below Mt. Bonnell, fighting the urge to scrach the prickly heat croppng up you know where. Pansy and Frank take Dad's Volvo to the lake. They park and Frank heaves air into the inflatable raft. Red-faced, asthmatic and soft as a jelly donut, Frank looks a lot like Pansy's daddy. He quaffs another Shiner Bock and Pansy eyes him sidelong. She looks swell in her bikini top and cut-offs. She lights another clove cigarette. Soon they are floating past the impressive cliffs. Frank, buoyant in this water element, paddles towards a secluded cove. He docks their tiny craft in a grove of madrones. "Nobody can see us here," he whispers. Pansy says nothing. She watches a skinny man pull out of the water and begin throwing himself up the overhanging wall. Near the top, thirty feet above the green lake, the man falters. He moans. His legs are shaking. "I'm not going to make it!" Then he plummets like a swooping hawk. His body splits the still surface. The water closes over his head. Pansy screams shrilly and Frank loses his ephemeral erection. "That was horrible," Pansy cries, "horrible, horrible, horrible!"

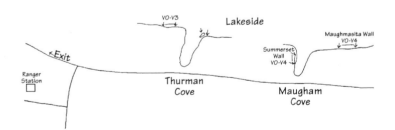

PACE BEND PARK OVERVIEW

Kevin Gallagher, Pace Bend   Photo by Scott Melcer

Maugham Cove

These excellent summer bouldering spots are located along the wall where rednecks frequently jump off (see map). Check for bone splintering landings by sounding the bottom. Serious boulderers will want a flotation device to double as a crash pad in shallow water and as a rest in deep water. Water levels drop continually throughout the summer, changing the nature of the routes. Access both walls by jumping in. On the Summerset Wall climb out over the big boulders on the north (left) end of the wall (5.6X) or swim back to Maugham Cove.

Thurman Cove

(Left to right)

1. Spider Baby 5.10- (Alvin Pons, Kirk Holladay. 4 bolts, anchors.)
2. ? 5.11c (Alvin Pons, Kirk Holladay. 5 bolts, anchors.)
3. Dude from Dallas 5.8 (Some dude from Dallas. 2 bolts, anchors.)

The following climbs can only be approached by boat. Ask the
    Crumpster for specific beta and a ride in his catamaran.

4. Head Boat 5.11+ Dave Head
5. Voyage of the Boat People 5.12 ₩ James Crump
6. Bay of Pigs 5.12 James Crump
7. Plight of the Haitian Refugees 5.10 James Crump
8. Traverse from Plight 5.10 James Crump

Marshall Cove

(Left to right)

1. 5.11- Kirk Holladay, Bill Gooch. 4 bolts, anchors.
2. Mysterious White Hand 5.9 Kirk Holladay, Bill Gooch. 30 yards right of 5.11a. 3 bolts, anchors.
3. 5.9 Kirk Holladay, Bill Gooch. 4 bolts, anchors.
4. 5.10 Kirk Holladay, Bill Gooch. 3 bolts, anchors.
5. 5.7 Kirk Holladay, Bill Gooch. 3 bolts, anchors. 20 yards right of 5.10.
6. 5.7 Kirk Holladay, Bill Gooch. 3 bolts, anchors.

San Antonio Limestone

San Antonio has a good amount of limestone. The cliffs along the Guadalupe have yielded many fine problems to folks like Alex Catlin, Joe Lowe, Liz Culbertson and Jacob Valdez. Cub Cave is developing into a great sport climbing venue and even as we speak, dear reader, more rock is being found, more bolts are being drilled and San Antonio climbers are hammering themselves on the anvil of limestone.

• *Point of Interest:* It's worth the drive to Elgin to pick up some scrumptious Hot Gut known to cure hangovers faster than you can say Jack Robinson.

• *Breakfast and Late Night:* Earl Abel's on Broadway

• *Coffee:* Pour La France, 7959 Broadway, 8264333

• *Beer:* The Liberty Bar is probably the best all around hang in San Antonio. Paper tablecloths are great for drawing topo's. 328 East Josephine, 227-1187. Suny's on St. Mary's (The majority of San Antonio's bars are along St. Mary's. What would Mary think about that?)

• *Vegetarian:* Gini's Home Cooking and Bakery on 7214 Blanco near 410. 342-2768. Twin Sisters Bakery and Cafe on 6322 North New Braunfels (just off Broadway). 822-0761

• *Carnivore:* E. Z.'s on Broadway right next to Twin Sisters.

• *Groceries:* Sun Harvest on Blanco across from Gini's offers good stuff, good for you. H. E. B., Albertson's on Broadway.

• *Gear:* Mursch Sports. See Yellow Pages for new address.

• *Camping:* Guadalupe State Park.

Guadalupe River Cliffs (AKA The Academy)

Route 474 Access

Directions: CLOSED

The Dire Wall

(left to right)

Problems start as low as possible. One of the best bouldering areas in Central Texas.

1. V9 Traverse (project)
2. V0 Iron cross that starts at the edge of overhanging rock on the left.
3. MFMF V1 Dyno to hueco. Classic.
4. V1 Left to vertical crack. (V2 Direct).
5. V1 Vertical crack.
6. V1+ Right of crack on pockets.
7. V3 Lunge from diagonal edge. Climb through the large hueco.
8. Roller Girl V4 Use the hand-sized hueco.
9. Immoralist V4 Wildly overhanging with edges.
10. Moraline V4 Just before the lower roof, follow three good pockets to a lunge.
11. The Asetic V? Use the sloping dish right of Moraline.
12. Antichrist V? Out left side of roof.
13. God V7 Diagonal out the roof to the right, then up to a large hueco.
14. Gabriel V5 Thin seam with worms. Starts at the back of the roof.)
15. Sultans of Swing 5.10+ Alex Catlin (Traverse out the left side of the roof and up. First ascent soloed then retro-bolted. 2 bolts.)
16. Confidential Information V2 R (Crank the roof just right of center. Necky.)
17. V0 Climb just left of a tree growing close to the cliff.

(Warm up area with numerous quality V0's at the right end of the wall.)

The Gallery

1. Black Satin 5.12 (2 bolts) Alex Catlin

2. The Dancer 5.12- (3 bolts) Alex Catlin (Right along the lip after the first bolt on Satin.)
3. Self Control 5.12+ (5 bolts) Alex Catlin (Start off boulder to left end of the roof. No Self Control—Left after the second bolt 5.11b.)
4. Slipstream 5.13- (5 bolts) Alex Catlin (Start off the boulder and climb through five bolts straight out.)
5. Jump Start 5.12 (4 bolts) Alex Catlin (Traverse right to small part of the roof. Straight out after second bolt is 5.12+.)
6. Velvet Green 5.12 (5 bolts) Alex Catlin (Start off the right end of the ledge. Follow a crack to the lip.)
7. The Teacher 5.13 (3 bolts) Alex Catlin (Start just right of Velvet.)

The Snake Roof
This bouldering roof is found 200 feet from the parking area on the way to the Greek Wall. It is divided into three sections.
1. Snake Left— Few holds. Fewer problems.
2. Center Snake— Seven problems from V2 to V6.
3. Snake Right-Left Edge V2, Center V2, Right Edge V0

The Greek Wall
(Walk downstream along the south bank.)
1. Agamemnon 5.13 (Hard start to a series of four pockets. Way over hung.)
The Cap, a 20 foot boulder that sits directly above the cliff, marks the center of the Achilles Wall.
2. Hector 5.10 Liz Culbertson (Bolts. Series of pockets to a verticle blank section at the top)
3. Odysseus 5.11 TR (Left of Hector)
4. Cyclops 5.11 TR (Steep pockets to a pair of pockets in a blank section, then through a blank roof.)
5. Pandora's Box 5.11 Alex Catlin (Right side of bulging roof past 2 bolts)
6. Earthly Desires 5.10+ Joe Lowe (2 bolts. Left side of bulging roof.)

Variation 5.12- (Crank center of roof.)

7. Patroklus (AKA Fag Roof) 5.11- Joe Lowe (3 bolts. Right end of Central Achilles Wall.)
8. Bristes 5.13 TR (5 feet left of Patroklus)
9. Achilles 5.13 TR (Follow pockets to the right side of the Cap, move right, then through two roofs. One bolt.)
10. Helen's Slot 5.12- Alex Catlin (Slot under left side of the Cap.)
11. Cerebrus (Mantel from Hell) 5.11 (Up to the obvious sloping dish)
12. Lycoon Roof V1 Right side of low roof. Snakes.
13. Arete V3 Left side of Lycoon Roof

The Wall Without a Name

(Downstream from the Greek Wall. Walk past a mossy wall to an open field. The Wall is a clean, slightly overhanging wall in the field, below a trailer park.)

1. Route Without a Name 5.11- Joe Lowe (Edges fifteen feet left of the double cracks. No pro.)

The Herniator Wall

(Across the river and slightly downstream from the Greek Wall. Excellent bouldering with bolts. Twenty minute approach.)

1. The Herniator 5.12 (3 bolts.) Alex Catlin (Left end of the steep wall)
2. Tecna-colored Groan 5.13 (Good pocket to a bagel, iron cross left and up.)
3. Warm Vomit 5.13- (3 bolts. Right of Tecna.)
4. Chunks 5.13- (Pockets right of Warm Vomit)
5. Mud Streaks 5.13 Alex Catlin (3 bolts. Start in the big hueco on the right side of the wall.)
6. Unexpected Inflamation 5.12 (Eight feet right of Mud Streaks.)
7. Jacob's Roof 5.13 (crack)
8. The Vicious Creation 5.13- (20 feet right of Jacob's. Start at the pinky pocket.)

The Dog Beater Walls

(Just past the Herniator Wall and slabs, the not-quite-so-overhanging walls.)

1. Wok the Dog 5.10c Alex Catlin (Yellow corner to the woof!)
2. The Dog Beater 5.11 (Overhanging right-facing corner.)
3. Puppy Slush 5.12- Alex Catlin (Arete right of Dog Beater. No pro.)
4. Choke the Puppy 5.12- Alex Catlin (1 bolt. Crack and overhanging arete 30 feet right of Puppy Slush.)
5. The Dog House 5.12 Alex Catlin (2 bolts, joins Choke at the 2nd Bolt.)

ROUTE 3160 ACCESS

Directions: CLOSED

Access: Temperamental landowner owns a firearm. Closed, closed, closed.

Punk Boulders

(Walk up river on the north bank. Pass sharp problems and arrive at a cave. Fifteen to twenty foot wall, half a mile long with "countless good problems.")

1. Scary Roof V1 (Way left.)
2. Pockets V2 (Right leaning diagonal seam.)
3. Climb V3 (10' right of seam.)
4. Undercling V2 (Roof hueco to dyno.)
5. Central Roof V7 (Right side of central roof. V4 from first hole.)
6. Large Holes V2 (Right of roof.)

Funk Wall

(Downstream on south bank. Forty to fifty foot wall that runs for a mile.)

1. Psycho Therapy 5.13+ TR (Obvious overhanging orange streak through a roof.)
2. Wall of Voodoo 5.12+ (3 bolts five feet left of Psycho.)
3. Radio Clash 5.11 TR (Thin crack in the dihedral.)
4. First Aid 5.9 TR (Shallow right corner 40' left of Radio.)
5. Route from Hell 5.12+ TR (Painful face.)

GUADALUPE STATE PARK

Directions: From Austin: I35 South to New Braunfels. Exit Highway 46 to Bourne. Stay on 46 for 27 miles. Turn onto Park Road 31 for three miles to the ranger station.

Ziggy Wall

(Unimposing twenty foot wall. Walk to the river from campsite #33 and turn upstream. All routes have three bolts unless otherwise indicated. All first ascents: Alex Catlin. Left to Right.)

1. See Emily Play 5.10 (2 bolts. Thin Crack.)
2. Quicksand 5.10+
3. Top Rope 5.11
4. Sorrow 5.11+ ♛ (To horizontal crack.)
5. Suffergette 5.12- (Large hueco at the lip.)
6. Spiders from Mars 5.11
7. Cracked Actor 5.11 (Less than vertical headwall.)
8. Lady Stardust 5.10 (Climbs same headwall as Actor.)
9. Time 5.12 (Hard moves through roof.)
10. Rat Race 5.12- (Just left of Time. Hard moves to a horizontal.)
11. Alladin Sane 5.12 (Lunge from a big square cut.)
12. Panic in Detroit 5.12-
13. Rosalyn 5.12 (4 bolts)
14. Kooks 5.12- (4 bolts)
15. Queen Bitch 5.12 (4 bolts)
16. Pretty Things 5.12 (4 bolts)

The Hero Wall

(Thirty foot, north facing wall. Continue upstream from the Ziggy Wall.)

1. Kreature 5.10- John Kressic (Any variation on the right end of the wall.)
2. Sons of the Silent Age 5.12 Alex Catlin (Pockets up and left to crack in the center of a roof.)
3. The Dome 5.13 Alex Catlin (Pockets up and right to left side of roof.)

4. Moonage Daydream 5.12- Alex Catlin (Rounded Arete)
5. Scary Monsters 5.12 Alex Catlin (Two holes seven feet left of Moonage to pockets.)
6. Blackout 5.12 Alex Catlin (Three finger pocket in yellow roof to small pocks above.)
7. The Beast V1 (Big hole in left end roof to hard lip move.)

281 Roof
(South side of the river, just downstream of hwy. 281. Landings are on a gravel bar that is sometimes submerged.)
1. Left Side V1 (Several warm-up problems.)
2. Left Edge V6 (Climb left edge of the roof on small pockets.)
3. Center V4
4. Crack V2 (Classic)
5. Little Roof (On the right. Landing is often wet.)

THE MEDINA

Directions: This area is CLOSED to climbing
Access: CLOSED.
General Description: The Medina offers the best potential for cutting-edge sport routes in all of Texas. Bullet rock. Thin pockets. Steeper than a new Mercedes. Perhaps one day we'll be allowed access to these radical bluffs so we can redpoint our projects.

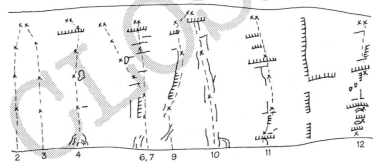

MEDINA LEFT

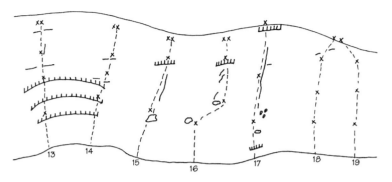

MEDINA RIGHT

(Left to Right)

1. Southrey's Paradise (Various Top Ropes 5.8 to 5.10)
2. Warm-up 5.9 Bolts, chain anchor. Alex & Elaine Catlin
3. Warm-up 5.10 Bolts, chain anchor. Alex & Elaine Catlin
4. Comanche Clip 5.12- Alex Catlin
5. Project
6. El Pinto 5.11+ El niño left variation. Josh Pierce.
7. El Niño 5.12- ₩₩ Jeb Vetters (Could be the best 12a in Central Texas.)
8. Project 5.13-
9. Counting Coup 5.13+ (Project)
9a. The Native 13+ (Project)
11. Braggadocio 5.13+ (Project)
11. Will To Power 5.13 (Alex Catlin)
12. Noble Savage 5.13 (Kevin Gallagher, Jeff Jackson)
13. The Breeder 5.13 (Project)
14. Komodo 5.13- (Alex Catlin)
15. Anolis 5.12 (Alex Catlin)
16. Scripto 5.12 (Jeff Jackson)
17. The Golooly 5.13- (Can be started sitting down. Jeff Jackson)
18. Nice 5.12- (Alex Catlin)
19. Toprope 5.12
20. Warm-up 5.10 (Elaine Catlin)

CUB CAVE

Directions: From Austin: I35 South to 46 West to 281 South. Just inside San Antonio city limits (past Mouses convenience store), turn right on Stone Creek Canyon. Right at Champion Stables. Take a left at the first gravel road. Park at the boulders and follow the trail downhill from your car to a cave hidden by trees.

General Description: Steep limestone cave.

Access: At last word, climbing was not restricted at this cave.

Camping: No camping at the cave, but Guadalupe State Park is approximately fifteen miles to the north on 281.

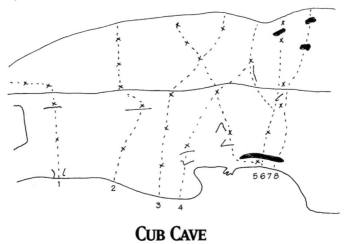

CUB CAVE

Cub Cave

(left to right)

1. White Trash 5.11 Alex Catlin
2. Fisher King 5.13- 👑 Mike Klein
3. Genetic Drift 5.12 👑 Jeb Vetters, Paul Erbe
4. Triple X Baby 5.12 Jeb Vetters
5. Bio Plasm 5.12 Jeb Vetters (Start atop boulder on left of lower cave.)
6. Thieving Texan Scum 5.13 Alex Catlin
7. Subterranean 5.12 Mike Klein
8. Dominion of Evil 5.13 Project (Start Subterranean, then straight out.)

9. Josh Pierce Can Climb It 5.10 Josh Pierce

Grand Dragonfly V3 (Start under Genetic and traverse left out of the cave. No heel hooks allowed.)

SAN ANTONIO METROPOLITAN AREA

Shavano Roof 5.11+

Directions: I 35 South to 1604 West. Take Northwest Military Highway (1535) South past De Zavala Road to Cliffside Drive. Take a left. After left bend, park and Shavano Roof is located just off the east side of the road.

General Description: Mike Lewis calls this, "The Grandpapa of San Antonio roof climbs."

Rolling Stone Wall

Directions: I 35 South to 1604 West. Take Northwest Military Highway (1535) South past De Zavala Road to Huebner Road. Take a left. Follow Huebner to Salado Creek and park. Rolling Stone Wall is found 150 yards south of Huebner on the west side of the creek.

General Description: Moderate, overhanging top-ropes. The Butch Roof V6 is located 100 feet to the right of the Rolling Stone Wall. This small, twenty foot roof problem comes highly recommended.

Olmos Wall and Olmos Dam Wall

Directions: CLOSED

General Description: Olmos Wall offers hardcore, man-made limestone traversing. Finger intensive with hard bouldering potential. Olmos Dam Wall sports a one hundred and fifty foot traverse and several excellent vertical problems from twelve to twenty five feet high. The perfect after-work climbing fix.

Pecos Limestone

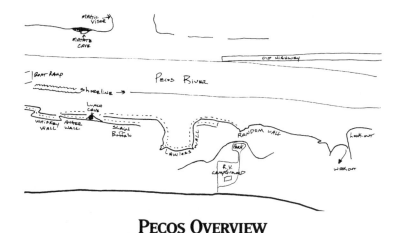

Pecos Overview

Pecos River Cliffs

Directions: Some people say you have to go through D'Hanis to get to d'cliffs. This is true only if you take I35 south to San Antonio and then take highway 90 west past Del Rio to the Pecos River. Other alternative routes exist and they avoid d'heinous D'Hanis. But they also take an hour longer from Austin.

General Description: The best moderate limestone climbing in Texas. Tall cliffs (up to 150'), bolted sport routes and naturally protected cracks. Bullet hard, featured limestone. Thanks to Alex Catlin, David McArthur, John Gogas, Carol Spoerl, Mike Lewis and Jacob Valdez for spraying in lines several years back. Other first ascents are credited in the text.

Camping: Camp at Seminole Canyon State Park, one mile east of the Pecos on I90. Home to some of the finest rock art in North America. You can't explore the canyon alone. Tours begin at 10 am and 3 pm and consist of a one mile guided hike. No rock throwing. Pets on leash only. No alcoholic beverages. Walking on trails only. Camping in designated areas only. No climbing.

Food: El Matador Restaurant located 15 minutes east of the Pecos on I90 in Comstock serves up awe inspiring soft chicken tacos for $4.75 and healthy bean chalupas (ask for soft tortillas). Closes early on Sunday night. Get beer at the Owl's Nest on the south side of I90 before Comstock. Good, cheap breakfast at The Seminole Inn, open early and for dinner when they have waitresses. Find the rest in Del Rio, 45 miles east of the Pecos.

Access: Stickey. There are those that would close these remarkable canyons to everyone in order to protect the pictographs. The Rock Art Foundation, for example, has installed a chainlink fence, padlocked and topped with barbed wire around the entrance to the White Shaman cave. Climbing, of course, is not tolerated.

The experts hypothesize that the White Shaman cave was the location for vision quests and peyote rituals where the participants would leave their bodies to communicate with the spirits. The rock art suggests this and so does the location. High above the canyon floor, a precarious path winds up the steep rock. You can still discern the polished path and even climb it, a steep 5.2. More than the ambiguous art, this bold approach suggests to those in the know that the White Shaman Cave was a place only visited by the bravest warriors in search of enlightenment. Ironically, this canyon, once home to a race of climbers, is now closed to rockclimbing. A cement staircase leads to the cave, steel railing sunk in the stone. The climber's approach, once such an integral part of the cave has been defiled forever. Why can't the people in charge see that rockclimbing is a connection between ourselves and those who have gone before?

Far from vandalism, climbing is a communion with nature, a ritual and an art. These caves and canyons were alive with people for thousands of years. Isn't it incongruous to restrict access to our primal home? They say that they are protecting the ancient art, but a chainlink fence and a padlock does nothing to deter vandalism. The fence is easily scaled. In fact, the fence is the symbol that vandals are addressing. Everyone should be welcome to visit the sacred sites. Free access would give the vandals nothing to trasnsgress. Free access would rob their acts of meaning.

Fences, rules and restrictions; there are far too many of these in our wilderness areas.

Wayne Crill, *Dancing With Too Many Girls* 5.12   Photo by Benji Fink

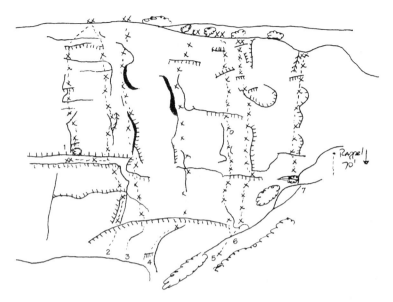

RANDOM WALL

Random and Lawless Walls

Access: Before climbing at the Random and Lawless, check in with Sue at the Chevron on the south-east side of the river. Sign a release and don't wax poetic on the Dallas Cowboys. Sue is a Redskin fan.

Directions: Drive south along the east bank of the Pecos and park at the Pecos River Campground (it might be closed, if so, park at the entrance). Walk to the right (north) side of the parking lot and follow a trail towards the river that leads to a picnic table and fire ring. Top anchors for The Random Wall are located directly behind the table. To find the Lawless, follow a left-tending trail out of the picnic clearing and walk to the edge of the cliff. Look for top anchors on this west-facing alcove. Parts of the Lawless get shade all day.

Rappel to access both areas. The Random Wall is 150' tall and can not be accessed with one doubled rope.

Random Wall

(left to right)

1. All This Way for the Short Ride 5.11+ (Start Well Tuned and veer left

to anchors. Belay here and continue up.)

2. Well Tuned Evinrude 5.11+
3. Bucket Rider 5.11
4. Smoking Guns 5.12-
5. He Drove Porches 5.11 (16 bolts)
6. She Rode Horses 5.11 (18 bolts, cuts right from He Drove.)
7. Humping the Camel 5.10 (First climb left of gully.)

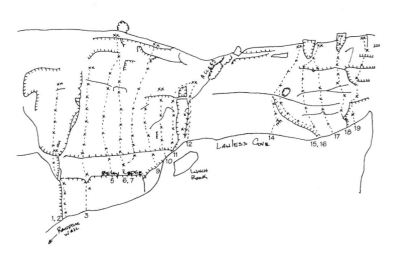

LAWLESS WALL

Lawless Wall

(left to right)

Cresent Conundrum 5.11- Martin Monroe (Around the corner left of
Texas Two Step.)

1. Texas 2-Step ♛5.9 (Bolted crack.)
2. Dancing With Too Many Girls 5.12- (Continuation of 2-Step. Beautiful
pocket-face. Desperate clips.)
3. Chimney Sweep 5.10- (Obvious dihedral.)
4. The Real U. T. is in Tennessee ♛ 5.10-
5. Wetback Expressway ♛ 5.9
6. Scott Free 5.10-

7. Hanging Judge 5.10-
8. Low Angle Face 5.7 (Starts off the belay ledge above the following four routes.)
9. Andy's Encore 5.12- ♕
10. Running From the Law ♕ 5.12-
11. Fool's Way Out* 5.11-
12. The Way Out ♕ ♕ 5.9+
13. Zoo Warm-up V0 - V3 (Lovely, shaded traverse cave.)
14. Basta 5.13+ ♕
15. Wrangler Savvy ♕ ♕ 5.11 (Moves left of tree. Soopurb!)
16. Cow Smarts 5.8+
17. Giddy-up 5.10- (Shares anchor with Cow Smarts.)
18. War Path 5.11 ♕ (Great climbing, but strangely bolted.)
19. Jurisdiction 5.11+ ♕ ♕

Further down . . .
20. Monopoly 5.10 (Downhill from Jurisdiction.)
21. 5.7 ♕ ♕ (Next bolted climb downhill from Monopoly.)
22. 5.8 (Crack with TR anchors. Find anchors by scrambling through a cave uphill from Monopoly.)
23. Coup Stick 5.13, 5.12 ♕ ♕ Jeff Jackson (1st pitch climbs the black, pocketed face to a sloping ledge. 2nd pitch pulls the roof.)

"How much one is able to endure: distress, want, bad weather, sickness, toil, solitude. Fundamentally one can cope with everything else, born as one is to a subterranean life of struggle; one emerges again and again into the light, one experiences again and again one's golden hour of victory — and then one stands forth as one was born, unbreakable, tensed, ready for new, even harder, remoter things, like a bow that distress only serves to draw tauter."

— Friedrich Nietzsche, On the Genealogy of Morals

Jonathan Anderson, *Running from the Law* 5.12-

Photo by Benji Fink

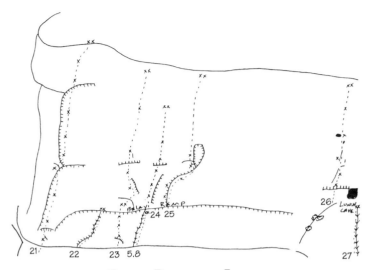

SLAIN BUFFALO LEDGE

Slain Buffalo Ledge

The following climbs are located along the large ledge up and right of the first pitch of Coup Stick. This ledge is distinguished by a crack system that outlines the shape of a buffalo. Red stains below the buffalo suggest blood. This landmark not only resonates with the recent history of buffalo extermination, but also recalls the Mass Kill methods of the ancient Native Americans. Entire herds of animals were driven off the edges of these very cliffs and used as food by the Indians. About 8,000 years ago these mass kills resulted in food shortages and starvation — an early example of mankind's rapacious utilization of natural resources.

Coup Stick 5.12 (2nd pitch begins on left side of Slain Buffalo Ledge.)

24. Cat on a Hot Tin Roof 5.12 ₩ ₩ (Super! Arching crack.)

25. Medicine Wheel 5.13 ₩ (Arching crack right of Cat.)

26. Flaming Arrow 5.12- ₩ Kevin Gallagher (Climbs the steep face 100' right of Medicine, directly above the obvious Lunch Cave.)

27. 5.7 (Climbs crack to anchors below Flaming.)

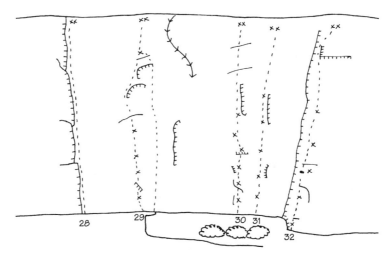

WHISKEY WALL

Whiskey Wall

This wall is located 100 yards right of Lunch Cave.

27a. Anomaly 5.11+ ₩ Kevin Bentz

28. 5.7 (Obvious crack with TR anchors.)

28a. Stab it and Steer 5.11- Sherry Cole

29. 5.10 ₩ (Bolts and anchors.)

29a. Frosted Flake 5.10 Kevin Bentz

29b. Tugboat Granny 5.9+ Martin Monroe

29c. Spike Shabook 5.10- Martin Monroe

30. 5.11 ₩ (Bolts and anchors.)

31. The Bear Paw 5.11 ₩ Rick Watson

32. Shaman in a Bottle 5.12 ₩ Jeff Jackson & Kevin Gallagher
(Obvious arete right of Bear.)

Shaman Wall

(Left to Right)

33. Dwarf Shaman 5.13 (This fierce power problem is located just right of Shaman in a Bottle.)

34. Uber Shaman 5.12 ₩ Jeff Jackson

35. Shamaroid 5.13 Alex Catlin (Project)

36. Sky Shaman 5.13- ⚕ Alex Catlin

37. Geisha Man 5.12 ⚕ Alex Catlin (Right of dihedral.)

Metalogic Wall

38. Aporia 5.12 ⚕ Elizabeth Culbertson

39. Terry's Project 5.12

40. Metalogic 5.14 (Project)

41. Reading Iculus 5.13 (Project)

Dock Wall

41a. Coyote Trickster Martin Monroe (Left of concrete butress)

42. Conjur It Up 5.12 Jeff Jackson, Jonathon Anderson, Benji Fink

PECOS RIVER CLIFFS
A.K.A. ROCK ART FOUNDATION CLIFFS

Directions: NO CLIMBING.

These cliffs are located on the land across the road from the Chevron station.

Access: There is NO CLIMBING at this site, The White Shaman Preserve. You can, however, tour the site with a ranger in tow by joining the Rock Art Foundation. Call Jim Zintgraff in San Antonio at (210) 525-9907 for details and application materials. The Rock Art Foundation was founded to protect and preserve the incredible pictographs found along the Pecos River. In the past, climbing was allowed here. Let's hope that these amazing cliffs will be open to climbing again soon.

Dead Pool

(southeast wall)

The area around the Dead Pool, a lovely seep and pool festooned with Anazazi handprints, is currently CLOSED to climbing and bouldering.

1. Dead Ringer 5.9 (Left line, 2 bolts and top anchors.)

2. Dead Poet Society 5.10 (Right line, 2 bolts and anchors.)
3. Grateful Dead Boulder V1 (Climb the uphill side of the first boulder down from the pool.)

Access the other areas by walking up the northwest side of the canyon and along the rim of the cliff that borders the Pecos. The rappel/top-rope anchors are a little difficult to locate.

Jungle Wall
(right to left)
1. Concrete Jungle 5.12- (Top-rope, top anchors at 50'.)
2. Welcome to the Jungle ♔ 5.11 (Marked by a right, diagonal flake and high first bolt. 4 bolts, anchors, 50'.)
3. Junglar 5.12 (Start up Welcome and move right after 20' into over hanging roofs and scoops.)
4. Jungle Book 5.7 (Dihedral. Nuts and Freinds. 80'.)
5. Jungle Bunny 5.11- (Start in the hand crack 60 yards west of Jungle Book. Top-rope, anchors, 85'.)

Brewski Wall
(right to left)
1. Sud Sucker 5.11+ (Climb the right most crack and veer right. Top rope, top anchors and directional, 75'.)
2. Tour de Lite 5.11 (Climb the left crack and move right across two other cracks. Pull the roof via the large knob. Top rope, top anchors and directional, 75'.)
3. Silver Bullet 5.11- (Climb the finger crack to the arete. Top rope, anchors, 75'.)
4. Vaginal Discharge 5.9 (4 bolts, anchors, 80'.)

The Cheese Wall
(right to left)

The climbs on this wall flank a large, rotten roof.

1. Hipmotize ☙ 5.10- (Right side of the cheezy roof. 7 bolts, top anchors, 100')
2. Master of Disaster 5.12- (Top rope the overhang to a thin crack in a dihedral, 100'.)
3. Pecos Shuffle 5.9 ☙ (Left of the cheezy roof. 6 bolts, top anchors, 80'.)
4. Shuffle Direct 5.11 (Top rope straight up from the first bolt on the Shuffle.)
5. Slam Dance 5.11- (Top rope the left diagonal crack, right of Shuffle.)

The Bullet Wall
(right to left)
Walk the edge of the cliff past a fence. Rappel into the Bullet Wall using any of the top anchors. The first set of anchors past the fence is Naked Gun 5.10c.

1. Misfire ☙ 5.11- (Ascend the face on the right side of the buttress. 7 bolts, anchors, 75'.)
2. Line of Sight 5.11 (Left side of buttress. 5 bolts, anchors, 65'.)
3. Lady Remington 5.10- Mike Lewis (Start on left angling cracks. 5 bolts, anchors, 65'.)
4. Hanging Judge 5.11 Mike Lewis (Left-most climb on the buttress. Start in the dihedral. 4 bolts, anchors, 70'.)
5. Naked Gun 5.10 Mike Lewis (6 bolts, anchors, 80'.)
6. Pop Gun 5.10- John Kresic (Climb the flake and pull the roof left of Naked. 5 bolts, anchors, 80'.)
7. Reactive Armor ☙ 5.11 Jacob Valdez (Marked by a pin driven behind a flake. 6 bolts, anchors, 80'.)
8. Disarmed 5.11 Jacob Valdez (Very technical. 6 bolts missing hangers. Anchors. 80'.)
9. Sticky Sweet ☙ 5.11+ Jacob Valdez (Friction. 8 bolts, anchors, 80'.)
10. Crossburn 5.12 Jacob Valdez (Climb to a left angling crack. Pimp desperate sidepulls. 7 bolts, anchors, 80'.)

11. Crossfire 5.11+ Jacob Valdez (Start at Crossburn and climb the left angling crack. Head right to finish Crossburn. 6 bolts, anchors, 80'.)

12. Powderburn 5.12 Jacob Valdez (Get the Crossfire undercling and go straight up. 7 bolts, anchors, 80'.)

13. Suppressor 5.12 Jacob Valdez (Thin pockets. 7 bolts, anchors, 80'.)

14. Heat Seeker ☝ 5.11+ Jacob Valdez (Right-facing crack/corner. 7 bolts, anchors, 80'.)

15. Bulletproof ☝ 5.12- Alex Catlin (Start in the thin, left-facing dihedral. Ascend pockets and bullet holes. 5 bolts, anchors, 80'.)

16. Gun Control 5.12 (Top rope, anchors, 80'.)

17. American Roulette 5.13 (Top rope, anchors, 80'.)

A break occurs in the wall.

18. Lawyers, Guns and Money 5.11 (Top rope the thin crack line. Anchors, 75'.)

19. Flakey Leonard 5.10 (8 bolts, anchors, 75'.)

Way left.

20. Nintendo ☝ 5.11+ Jacob Valdez (6 bolts, anchors, 75'.)

21. No-name 5.7 (Top rope, 40'.)

22. No-mane 5.8 (Top rope, 45'.)

The Noon Wall
(right to left)
Round the left corner of the Bullet Wall to find this steep, shady grotto.

1. Splinter ☝ ☝ 5.11- (4 bolts, anchors, 60'.)

2. Shredder ☝ ☝ 5.10 Alex Catlin (4 bolts, shares anchors with Splinter, 55')

3. Cowabunga ☝ 5.13 Alex Catlin (Top rope left of Shredder. Rumored to have fixed anchors.)

"There are only three sports — mountain climbing, bull fighting, and motor racing — all others being games."

— Ernest Hemingway

From Mike Lewis' Essay "The Golden Days"

"The morning sky is like molten lava, colored fire through the wispy clouds. You lay awake at dawn facing the east in your Mexican hammock. This light show is part of the reason you love it here. This is the land of Roy Bean's law, two miles from water and two feet from hell. An early start is the only way to start here. The mornings are nice and clear but the afternoon is like a reflector oven. Sometimes you think about the effort. Why is this place so difficult yet strangely attractive? It has an appeal, a lore all it's own. The ancient Indians lived here, survived here. Their lore is all around and you can feel it. Something basic, early man, an instinctual attraction seemingly common to most climbers. The obvious mundane response is that the rock climbing is goooood. Oh yeah, its good, but there is more. The mystique of this place is not for everyone, and few would call this apparent wasteland anything but worthless. But those who cannot see or will not see are destined to frequent the suburban sprawl and turnstiles of popular areas . . . . Our predecessors have left indelible impressions on many of the sacred walls. As you wander through the area, you become a part of their legacy, a part of the history of this remarkable place. A place for action and endurance, yet introspection. These intangible qualities are lucid to those who frequent this land. The mystique of this place is it's history and it's history is now."

Top Secret: Sitting Bull Falls, New Mexico

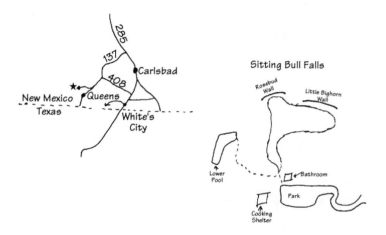

1. Fire Water 5.10a
2. Wounded Knee 5.10b
3. Six Little Indians 5.10c
4. Big Medicine 5.11c
5. Un-named 5.11b

6. Smoke Signals 5.11b
7. Ghost Dancer 5.12a
8. Counting Coop 5.12b
9. Eagles Don't Have To Be Crows 5.12b
10. Tribal Wars 5.12d
11. So Many Arrows 5.12d
12. Custard's Last Stand 5.13b

Leads by Grade

5.14-
Braggadocio (Medina) 101
Metalogic (Pecos) 113

5.13+
Finnegan's Wake (Bull Creek) 51
Counting Coup (Medina) 101
Medicine Wheel (Pecos) 111

5.13
Hieroglyphics (Cleburn) 22
Remus (Cleburn) 21
The Insulter (Cleburn) 24
The Albatross (Cleburn) 24
Desert Storm (Miller Springs) 31
The Chronic (Miller Springs) 33
Desert Shield (Miller Springs) 31
Wrath (Miller Springs) 33
Septic (Miller Springs) 33
Journeyman (Miller Springs) 33
Daddy Rain (Bucket Cave) 45
Slacker (Bucket Cave) 48
Bonzo's Revenge (Bull Creek) 51
Kubla Khan (Bull Creek) 51
Disneyland (New wall) 66
Plate Techtonics (Urban Assault) 71
Deep Flow (Urban Assault) 72
Lucky Strikes (Reimer's) 77
Reptile (Reimer's) 87
Wild Spider (Reimer's) 87
House of Pain (Reimer's) 88

Elephant Man (Reimer's) 77

Coletrane (Reimer's) 78

Mud Streaks (Gaudalupe) 96

Agamemnon (Guadalupe) 96

Bristes (Guadalupe) 97

Achilles (Guadalupe) 97

The Dome (Guadalupe) 99

Noble Savage (Medina) 101

The Breeder (Medina) 101

Will To Power (Medina) 101

Thieving Texas Scum (Cub Cave) 102

Dwarf Shaman (Pecos) 112

Reading Iculus (Pecos) 113

Shamaroid (Pecos) 113

American Roulette (Pecos) 116

Basta (Pecos) 109

Cowabunga (Pecos) 116

Coup Stick (Pecos) 109

5.13-

Lizard King (Cleburn) 23

Mariner (Cleburn) 24

Monogun (Cleburn) 24

Romulus (Cleburn) 21

Mr. Sir (Miller Springs) 33

Gulliver's Travels (Bull Creek) 51

Femme (Urban Assault) 71

Head (Reimer's) 77

Slipstream (Guadalupe) 96

The Teacher (Guadalupe) 97

Warm Vomit (Guadalupe) 97

Komodo (Medina) 101

The Golooly (Medina) 101
Fisher King (Cub Cave) 102
Sky Shaman(Pecos) 113

5.12+
Bone Sheath (Cleburn) 23
Mainstay (Cleburn) 24
Project Dog (Cleburn) 23
The Minotaur (Cleburn) 22
De La Soul (Miller Springs) 31
Raison d'etre (Miller Springs) 31
Metaphysics (Bull Creek) 51
Frank's Direct (Frank's Meat Market) 57
Dragonfly (Reimer's) 87
Bongo Direct (Reimer's) 87
Bay of Pigs (Thurman Cove) 93
Self Control (Guadalupe) 96
Bio Plasm (Cub Cave) 102
Subterranean (Cub Cave) 102

5.12
Disney Fignus (Plano Pyramids) 9
Arch de Triumph (Trammel Trestle) 14
Archetype (Cleburn) 24
Blitzkrieg (Cleburn) 23
Blue Velvet (Cleburn) 23
Drunken Boat (Cleburn) 22
Lust For Life (Cleburn) 22
Omen (Cleburn) 21
One Adam Twelve (Cleburn) 24
Painted Bird (Cleburn) 22
Calcutta Bunghole (Cleburn) 23

Rodeo On The Brazos (Cleburn) 22
Serpent And The Rainbow (Cleburn) 21
The Drone (Cleburn) 23
Concentrics (Miller Springs) 31
Semantics (Miller Springs) 31
Kinetics (Miller Springs) 31
The Gauntlet (Miller Springs) 33
Misery (Miller Springs) 31
Primadonna (Miller Springs) 31
Pocket Envy (Miller Springs) 33
Cosmic Thang (Miller Springs) 33
Steel Wheels (Miller Springs) 33
Bronco (Bull Creek) 51
Atlas Shrugged (Bull Creek) 51
Altered States (Bull Creek) 50
Lord of the Flies (Bull Creek) 51
Surrender (Bull Creek) 51
Holy Diver (Barton Creek) 64
Power Vision (New Wall) 67
Power Monkey (New Wall) 67
Iron Man (New Wall) 66
Hug Thy Mother (New Wall) 66
Mah Jong (Urban Assault) 71
Man Child (Urban Assault) 72
Masada (Urban Assault) 71
Starfish (Urban Assault) 71
Medicine Man (Urban Assault) 71
Mandibles (Urban Assault) 72
Rust Never Seeps (Reimer's) 82
Alvin's (Reimer's) 78
Learning To Fly (Reimer's) 78
No Recess (Reimer's) 78

Learning to Crawl (Reimer's) 78
Love Is A Fist (Reimer's) 78
Repulsive Attila (Reimer's) 78
Body Wax (Reimer's) 77
Learning to Crawl (Reimer's) 78
Love Shack (Reimer's) 84
Rain Dance (Reimer's) 88
Stranglehold (Reimer's) 88
Industrial Disease (Reimer's) 89
Voyage of the Boat People (Thurman Cove) 93
Aladdin Sane (Guadalupe) 99
Scary Monsters (Guadalupe) 100
Black Satin (Guadalupe) 95
Jump Start (Guadalupe) 96
Velvet Green (Guadalupe) 96
Rosalyn (Guadalupe) 99
Queen Bitch (Guadalupe) 99
Pretty Things (Guadalupe) 99
Blackout (Guadalupe) 100
Sons of the Silent Age (Guadalupe) 99
Anolis (Medina) 101
Scripto (Medina) 101
Toprope (Medina) 101
Genetic Drift (Cub Cave) 102
Shaman In A Bottle (Pecos) 112
Geisha Man (Pecos) 113
Aporia (Pecos) 113
Suppressor (Pecos) 115
Terry's Project (Pecos) 113
Conjur It Up (Pecos) 113
Powderburn (Pecos) 115
Uber Shaman (Pecos) 112

123 LEADS BY GRADE

Cat On A Hot Tin Roof (Pecos) 111
Coup Stick (Pecos) 109
Crossburn (Pecos) 115
Dancing With Too Many Girls (Pecos) 108
Gun Control (Pecos) 116
Junglar (Pecos) 114

5.12-
The Decimator (Cleburn) 22
War Of The Worlds (Cleburn) 23
Turn Of The Screw (Cleburn) 24
Scarface (Cleburn) 22
Monkey Shines (Cleburn) 22
New Chipped Route (Cleburn) 25
Aqualung (Cleburn) 24
Black Rain (Cleburn) 24
Hey Zeus (Cleburn) 24
Pocket Pussy (Cleburn) 21
Ass Bar (Miller Springs) 31
Zenith (Miller Springs) 33
Roofus (Miller Springs) 33
Green Fuse (Bull Creek) 52
Boss Bull (Bull Creek) 52
Raging Bull (Bull Creek) 52
Beans and Rice (Bull Creek) 51
Do The Right Thing (Bull Creek) 51
Blatant AKA Head Trip (Bull Creek) 51
Tree of Woe (Mount Bonnell) 55
Ecbatana (Mt. Bonnell) 55
Nineveh (Mt. Bonnell) 55
Eraser Head (New Wall) 65
Buddha (New Wall) 65

Tunnel Vision Direct (New Wall) 66
Eye of the Storm (New Wall) 66
Space Cowboy (New Wall) 67
Running Man (Gus Fruh) 68
Liposuction (Reimer's) 77
Bad Language (Reimer's) 81
Nuerotica (Reimer's) 83
Punctuation Mark (Reimer's) 81
Rhetoric (Reimer's) 81
Let Them Eat Flake (Reimer's) 77
Grip Clip (Reimer's) 82
Incredible Journey (Reimer's) 82
Ship of Fools (Reimer's) 87
Power Pig (Reimer's) 87
Velcro Rodeo (Reimer's) 88
Earthly Desires Var. (Guadalupe) 96
Helen's Slot (Guadalupe) 97
Puppy Slush (Guadalupe) 98
The Dancer (Guadalupe) 96
Suffergate (Guadalupe) 99
Rat Race (Guadalupe) 99
Time (Guadalupe) 99
Panic In Detroit (Guadalupe) 99
Kooks (Guadalupe) 99
Moonage Daydream (Guadalupe) 100
Comanche Clip (Medina) 101
Nice (Medina) 101
El Niño (Medina) 101
Running From The Law (Pecos) 109
Smoking Guns (Pecos) 108
Flaming Arrow (Pecos) 111
Master Of Disaster (Pecos) 115

125 Leads By Grade

Bulletproof (Pecos) 116

Concrete Jungle (Pecos) 114

5.11+

Gandolf (Mineral Wells) 17

The French Connection (Cleburn) 21

Wild Planet (Cleburn) 21

Funky Comadina (Cleburn) 22

Minerva (Bull Creek) 51

High Times (Mount Bonnell) 55

Mandingo (New Wall) 65

Tunnel Vision (New Wall) 66

Jerry's Kids (Gus Fruh) 70

Dirty Rotten Whore (Beehive Wall) 75

Size Ain't Shit (Reimer's) 84

Mistaken Identity (Reimer's) 77

Head Boat (Thurman Cove) 93

El Pinto (Medina) 101

All This Way For The Short Ride (Pecos) 107

Andy's Encore (Pecos) 109

Crossfire (Pecos) 116

Well Tuned Evinrude (Pecos) 108

Heat Seeker (Pecos) 116

Jurisdiction (Pecos) 109

Nintendo (Pecos) 116

Sticky Sweet (Pecos) 115

Sud Sucker (Pecos) 114

Anomoly (Pecos) 112

5.11

Conquerette (Trammel Trestle) 14

Jesus Rules (Trammel Trestle) 14

Hidden Jewel (Mineral Wells) 17
Immigrant (Mineral Wells) 18
Keith's Way (Mineral Wells) 18
Dynamo Hum (Mineral Wells) 18
Cyclops (Cleburn) 22
Dirty Legs (Cleburn) 22
Kryptonite (Cleburn) 25
Willingjam (Cleburn) 22
The Obsession (Cleburn) 24
The Sorcerer (Cleburn) 25
Force Of One (Cleburn) 23
Gelfling Flakes (Cleburn) 23
Hopi Snake Dance (Cleburn) 23
Johnny Law (Cleburn) 24
Hyperactive (Miller Springs) 33
Bedtime For Bonzo (Bull Creek) 52
Gooched (Bull Creek) 52
Frank's Meat Market (Frank's) 57
Amputee Crack (University of Texas) 58
Tit Scratch (Barton Spings) 63
Head Trip (Barton Springs) 63
Gravity's Angel (Campbell's Hole) 64
Cloud Nine (New Wall) 65
Lots of People (New Wall) 65
Walk The Dog (New Wall) 65
Rabbit Hut (New Wall) 65
Heaven's Gate (New Wall) 66
Magical Mystery Tour (New Wall) 66
Girlie Vision (New Wall) 66
Reefer Madness (Gus Fruh) 68
Cyborg (Gus Fruh) 68
Sex Dwarfs (Gus Fruh) 70

Apostrophe (Gus Fruh) 69
Blind Date (Gus Fruh) 69
Ladrone (Urban Assault) 71
Cell Block (Urban Assault) 71
Spider Grind (Reimer's) 77
Mud Lip (Reimer's) 83
Tit For Tom (Reimer's) 83
Mas Cerveza (Reimer's) 86
Bongo Fury (Reimer's) 87
The Munchies(Reimer's) 89
Arete (Reimer's) 89
Beelzebubba (Reimer's) 83
Flea Circus (Reimer's) 82
Buttered Side Down (Reimer's) 86
Mother Buddha (Reimer's) 83
Sangre De Muertos (Reimer's) 78
Short Term Memory Loss (Reimer's) 89
Snuff The Rooster (Reimer's) 78
Underdog (Reimer's) 88
Ivy League (Reimer's) 88
Telegraph Road (Reimer's) 77
Crankenstein (Reimer's) 89
Pandora's Box (Guadalupe) 96
Patroklus (Guadalupe) 96
Sultans of Swing (Guadalupe) 95
Cerebrus (Guadalupe) 97
Cyclops (Guadalupe) 96
Spiders from Mars (Guadalupe) 99
She Rode Horses (Pecos) 108
Shuffle Direct (Pecos) 115
Tour De Lite (Pecos) 114
War Path (Pecos) 109

Welcome To The Jungle (Pecos) 114
Wrangler Savvy (Pecos) 109
The Paw (Pecos) 112
Reactive Armor (Pecos) 115
Disarmed (Pecos) 115
Bucket Rider (Pecos) 108
Hanging Judge (Pecos) 115
He Drove Porches (Pecos) 108
Lawyers, Guns And Money (Pecos) 116
Line Of Sight (Pecos) 115

5.11-
Finger Stinger (Mineral Wells) 16
Heat Seeker (Mineral Wells) 16
Frog Dance (Cleburn) 21
Gecko Man (Cleburn) 23
Blatty Crack (Cleburn) 21
Chemical Warfare (Bull Creek) 51
Balrog (Barton Springs) 63
Mr. Slate (New Wall) 65
Yabba Dabba Do (New Wall) 65
Hysteria (New Wall) 65
Wowie Zowie (New Wall) 65
Heaven Can Wait (New Wall) 66
Through the Looking Glass (New Wall) 66
Sunshine Boys (New Wall) 67
Rock and Roll High School (New Wall) 67
Trash-can Man (Gus Fruh) 69
Rock Retard (Gus Fruh) 69
Centipede (Reimer's) 79
Rags To Riches (Reimer's) 81
Cliptomania (Reimer's) 82

Bolt Talk (Reimer's) 86
Unnatural Selection (Reimer's) 87
Ant Encounters (Reimer's) 88
Teenage Parties (Reimer's) 88
Gang Bang (Reimer's) 89
Blowing Smoke At The Monkey (Reimer's) 86
Gangbang Offshoot (Reimer's) 89
Patroklus (Guadalupe) 97
Route Without a Name (Guadalupe) 97
Fool's Way Out (Pecos) 109
Cresent Conundrum (Pecos) 108
Misfire (Pecos) 115
Silver Bullet (Pecos) 114
Coyote Trickster(Pecos) 113
Slam Dance (Pecos) 115
Splinter (Pecos) 116

5.10+
Thieves and Assholes (Mineral Wells) 17
Cactus Jack (Cleburn) 24
Fatal Attraction (Cleburn) 23
Gay Bar Problem (Cleburn) 24
Gila Mama (Cleburn) 23
The Flying Dutchman (Cleburn) 21
Love On The Rocks (Cleburn) 23
Atomic Rush (Barton Springs) 63
Rocket Pocket (Barton Springs) 63
Schoolboy Fantasies (New Wall) 65
Cedar Fever (New Wall) 67
Birdland (Gus Fruh) 68
Charlie Don't Surf (Gus Fruh) 70
Urban Assault (Urban Assault) 72

Pay Dirt (Kirk And Alvin's Wall) 75
Pocket Rocket (Reimer's) 84
Digitron (Reimer's) 80
Pocket Change (Reimer's) 87
Crack Attack (Reimer's) 87
Wife in the Fast Lane (Reimer's) 89
Buttered Side Up (Reimer's) 86
Nobody's Hero (Reimer's) 82
Earthly Desires (Guadalupe) 99
Quicksand (Guadalupe) 99
Cracked Actor (Guadalupe) 99

5.10
Razor's Edge Roof (Renner Road) 12
Du Dihedral (Trammel Trestle) 14
Super Pro (Trammel Trestle) 14
Stylin' (Trammel Trestle) 14
Arete (Mineral Wells) 15
Thin Crack (Mineral Wells) 16
Bestard Climb (Mineral Wells) 16
5.10 Layback (Mineral Wells) 16
Apples to Hell (Miineral Wells) 16
The Short Unnamed (Mineral Wells) 17
Something In Between (Mineral Wells) 17
Two Fingers Tequilla (Mineral Wells) 17
Black Flag (Mineral Wells) 17
Right of Immigrant (Mineral Wells) 18
Under Immigrant (Mineral Wells) 18
Line Left (Mineral Wells) 18
Pee Wee's (Mineral Wells) 18
Moody Blues (Cleburn) 22
Armageddon (Cleburn) 21

Pegboard (Cleburn) 23
Planet X (Cleburn) 21
Snake Eyes (Cleburn) 21
Sundance (Cleburn) 23
Sweet Dreams (Cleburn) 20
Tai Chi (Cleburn) 22
Linda Blair A1 (Cleburn) 24
Deputy Dog (Cleburn) 24
King Jug (Cleburn) 21
Hippy Chick (Miller Springs) 31
Crack (Miller Springs) 31
Cripple Direct (University of Texas) 58
Last Picture Show (Mount Bonnell) 55
Rush (Barton Springs) 63
Crystal New Persuation (New Wall) 66
Gunsmoke (New Wall) 67
Hank's 5.10 (New Wall) 67
Gros Ventre (Gus Fruh) 68
Chicken Supreme (Gus Fruh) 69
Thumb Dance (Gus Fruh) 69
Praying Mantle (Gus Fruh) 69
Power Snatch(Reimer's) 79
Prototype (Reimer's) 86
Dead Cats (Reimer's) 79
Water Ballet (Reimer's) 80
Ferntasm (Reimer's) 82
T-roofic Detour (Reimer's) 82
War on Rugs (Reimer's) 88
Bluebeard (Reimer's) 83
Harelipped Dog (Reimer's) 83
Pika Peak (Reimer's) 84
Plight of the Haitian Refugees (Thurman Cove) 93

Lady Stardust (Guadalupe) 99
Hector (Guadalupe) 96
Warm-Up (Medina) 101
Warm-Up (Medina) 101
Naked Gun (Pecos) 115
Shredder (Pecos) 116
Monopoly (Pecos) 109
Dead Poet Society (Pecos) 114
Flakey Leonard (Pecos) 116
Humping The Camel (Pecos) 108

5.10 -
Magic Carpet Ride (Cleburn) 21
Strategic Arms (Cleburn) 21
Wedding Bells (Cleburn) 23
Torts (Mount Bonnell) 55
Zipper Lounge (Barton Springs) 63
Cactus Patch (New Wall) 66
King of Ging (Gus Fruh) 70
Gray Streak (Gus Fruh) 70
Reimerama (Reimer's) 79
Fearless (Reimer's) 82
Clone Call (Reimer's) 86
I Speak For The Trees (Reimer's) 87
Mikey Likes It (Reimer's) 83
Socks On Chicks (Reimer's) 86
Spider Baby (Pace Bend) 93
Hector (Guadalupe) 96
Kreature (Guadalupe) 99
Chimney Sweep (Pecos) 108
Hanging Judge (Pecos) 109
Giddy-Up (Pecos) 109

Hipmotize (Pecos) 115
Lady Remington (Pecos) 115
The Real U. T. Is In Tennessee (Pecos) 108
Pop Gun (Pecos) 115
Scott Free (Pecos) 108

5.9
Dark Man (Trammel Trestle) 14
Crumbly (Mineral Wells) 17
Connect The Pockets (Mineral Wells) 17
Green Variation (Mineral Wells) 17
5.9 Roof Routes (Mineral Wells) 18
Downhill Crack Traverse (Mineral Wells) 18
5.9 Variation (Mineral Wells) 18
Uphill Traverse (Mineral Wells) 18
Bad Dreams (Cleburn) 20
Trouble In River City (Cleburn) 22
Skeksis II (Cleburn) 22
Squaw Creek (Cleburn) 23
Agent Orange (Cleburn) 21
Chucks (Mount Bonnell) 55
Frank's Crack (Mount Bonnell) 55
Jester West Chimney (University of Texas) 58
Northside Dihedral (University of Texas) 59
Section 26 (University of Texas) 59
Northeast Sneak-in Crack (University of Texas) 59
Mosquito (Barton Springs) 63
Meet the Flintstones (New Wall) 65
Schoolboy Indirect (New Wall) 65
Tiddlywinks (New Wall) 66
Fern Bar (Gus Fruh) 68
Bulge (Gus Fruh) 70

April Fool (Gus Fruh) 70
Bloody Butt (Kirk And Alvin's Wall) 74
Skank Hole (Kirk And Alvin's Wall) 74
Let The Wallies Loose (Reimer's) 87
My Name Is Mud(Reimer's) 79
Smitten Psychopath (Reimer's) 85
Toilet Solo (Reimer's) 85
Almost Nothing To It (Reimer's) 79
Back Off Crack (Reimer's) 89
Bisector (Reimer's) 86
Tree (Reimer's) 87
Mysterious White Hand(Pace Bend) 93
First Aid (Guadalupe) 98
Warm-Up (Medina) 101
The Way Out (Pecos) 109
Texas 2-Step (Pecos) 108
Wetback Expressway(Pecos) 108
Pecos Shuffle(Pecos) 115
Dead Ringer (Pecos) 113

5.8

Offwidth Layback (Mineral Wells) 15
Arrow Flake (Mineral Wells) 15
George Hazzard Route (Mineral Wells) 15
Another Dave Problem (Mineral Wells) 16
Slap Roof (Mineral Wells) 16
In Search of Green (Mineral Wells) 17
Finger Crack (Mineral Wells) 18
Hilo Traverse (Mineral Wells) 18
Sandstone Roof (Mineral Wells) 18
5.8 Overhang (Mineral Wells) 18
Easy Face (Mineral Wells) 18

Constellation Bear (Cleburn) 21
Texas Constitution (Cleburn) 21
Mr. Cricket Goes To Washington A3 (Cleburn) 20
Rappeller's Wall (Barton Springs) 63
Wasp (Barton Springs) 63
Iranian Arms Deal (Gus Fruh) 68
Wyoming Women (Gus Fruh) 68
Right Face (5.8 Sanctuary) 74
Sanctuary Climbs (5.8 Sanctuary) 74
5.8 Flake (Reimer's) 86
Mega Lounge (Reimer's) 87
Dude From Dallas (Pace Bend) 93
Southrey's Paradise (Medina) 101
Cow Smarts (Pecos) 109
No-Mane (Pecos) 116

5.7
Track Crack (Trammel Trestle) 14
Practice Wall (Mineral Wells) 16
Short Easy Crack (Mineral Wells) 16
Hand Crack (Mineral Wells) 16
5.7+ Hand Crack (Mineral Wells) 17
Rewritten (Mineral Wells) 17
Roof Right of Mulberry (Mineral Wells) 17
Line Left of Mulberry (Mineral Wells) 17
Solo Crack (Mineral Wells) 18
Left Arete (Mineral Wells) 18
Tricam Crack (Cleburn) 20
Skeksis I (Cleburn) 22
Such A Flake (Cleburn) 24
Karen's Crack (Cleburn) 25
Kurt's Crack (Cleburn) 23

Right Wall (Cleburn) 20
Holtzendorf Direct (Barton Springs) 63
Terrace Access (New Wall) 65
Touch of Class (Gus Fruh) 70
Zoe's First Step (Reimer's) 78
Diehedral (Pecos) 112
Jungle Book (Pecos) 114
Low Angle Face (Pecos) 109
No-Name (Pecos) 109

5.6
Short Routes (Mineral Wells) 16
Easy Face (Mineral Wells) 17
Easy Wall (Mineral Wells) 18
Arete Solo (Mineral Wells) 18
Easy Crack (Mineral Wells) 18
B. P. Traverse (Mineral Wells) 18
Gay Bar Crack (Cleburn) 24
Indian Staircase Crack (Cleburn) 23
Mr. Cricket (Cleburn) 20
Perry Castenada Library Chimney (University of Texas) 58
New Wall Access (New Wall) 65
Flash Crack (Gus Fruh) 69
I Never Called You a Beast (Reimer's) 78
Maggie's Farm (Reimer's) 78
Teva Slab (Reimer's) 84

5.5
Big Offwidth (Mineral Wells) 16
Alaskan Crack (Mineral Wells) 16
Easy Tower (Mineral Wells) 17
Trash Crack (Mineral Wells) 17

Green Dihedral (Cleburn) 20
Thin Crack (Gus Fruh) 63

5.4
Diagonal (Cleburn) 23
Classic (Barton Springs) 63

5.2
Down Climb 5.2 (Mineral Wells) 17

The ultimate good is not to be afraid.

Frederich Nietzche

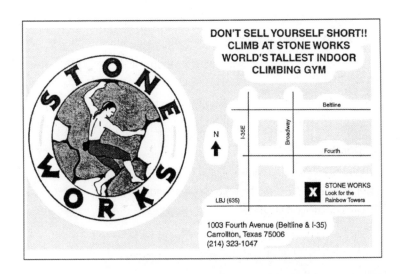

ADDENDUM TO REIMER'S FISHING RANCH

Reimer's Update:

The following information should clarify existing information and update route listings through November of 1995.

Addition: Serpent Wall

(Right to left) The serpent wall is located immediately on your right after you crest the rooty knoll on you way to the Dead Cats Wall. The routes start off a ledge.

24a. KB-5 5.11-

24b. KB-5 5.10

24c. Sidewinder 5.10 (Arete)

24d. 5.9 (Approximately 30' left of Sidewinder marked by obvious black hole)

Clarification:

24e. Hilti Highway 5.10 (Starts right of the two trees)

24f. Bolted Like Mex 5.10 (Climb seams starting between two trees)

25. Centipede

Clarification:

40. Ferntasm 5.10 (Obvious dihedral by large oak)

47. Nobody's Hero 5.10+ (Climbs the gray face on the right side of the large roofs well past Rust Never Seeps)

47a. Lucky's Longy 5.11+ Mike Klein (Starts 10' left of Hero and traverses under roof)

53. Mother Buddha (Located 15' right of the huge detached boulder)

To access the Hand Beyond Wall follow the path right along the cliff to next open area.

53a. Deception Path (Climbs up and through the right side of the roof)

54. Bluebeard (Starts at the large obvious handlebar)

54b. Antonioan (Dihedral)

54f. TR? (right of Daddy's Girl)

55. Daddy's Girl (Pocketed grey face 5' right of tree)

55a. Booger Boy (Starts next to tree.)

56. Hairlipped Dog (Located 30' left of Booger by a large boulder)

56b. San Antonio Rt. (Layback seam start)

56d. Another…5.10 (Starts off the tree)

56e. 5.10 (Left of Another)

56f. Shadowman 5.11- (Start on 3' shelf)

56g. Yet Another… (Starts just right of tufa features and tree)

Clarification: The Mai Tai Wall is located on the shelf located to the right of Prototype Wall.

79. Tree Route (Start at the tree)

80. Mega Lounge (30' to the right of tree route)

82a. Unknown 5.8 (Large detattched flake start right of I Speak…)

86-88 are as follows. These diffcult lines start just right of an obvious tree next to the cliff. Very steep!

86. Dragonfly 5.12+

86a. Klein's Project

87. Reptile (Black tufa project)

88. Wild Spider 5.13

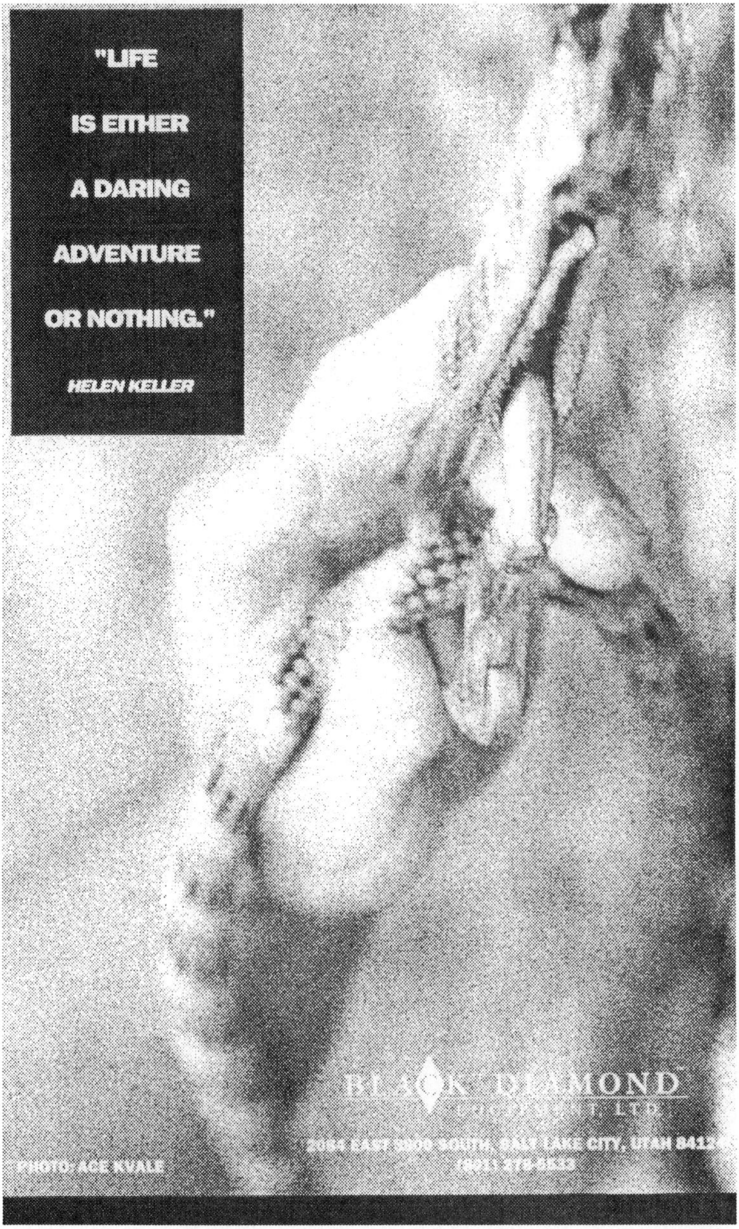
"LIFE
IS EITHER
A DARING
ADVENTURE
OR NOTHING."
HELEN KELLER
BLACK DIAMOND
PHOTO: ACE KVALE

BOMBPROOF
protection

is a summation of ingredients; sound rock, proper placement and quality equipment. Rest assured that when you place a Metolius 3 or 4 cam it will be as bomb-proof as the placement it's in! Climbers worldwide reach for Metolius Cams to help achieve their climbing goals - from the first free ascent of the Nose, to demanding alpine walls of the Himalaya. Let us help you to fully realize your outdoor climbimg adventures.

METOLIUS

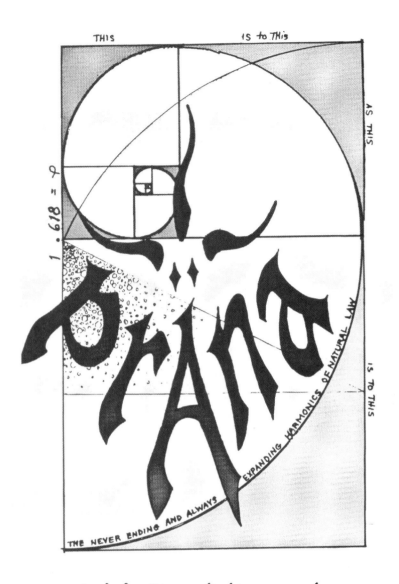

Look for Prana climbing apparel
at select climbing shops
around the world

6351 Corte Del Abeto A103 Carlsbad, CA 92009

619.431.8015